OUNDLE

AND THE
ENGLISH PUBLIC SCHOOL

School colours are awarded on the lawn in front of the Great Hall

O U N D L E

AND THE

ENGLISH PUBLIC SCHOOL

The Cloisters between lessons

RAYMOND FLOWER

S

STACEY

Editor Nicholas Drake
Art Director Keith Savage
Indexer Marie Lorimer

Oundle and the English Public School

First published 1989 by Stacey International
128 Kensington Church Street, London W8 4BH
Telex 298768 Stacey G
Fax 01-792 9288

Set in Goudy Old Style
by Capella D.T.P. Bureau, Stowmarket, Suffolk.
Printed and Bound in Singapore
by Tien Wah Press

British Library Cataloguing in Publication Data
Flower, Raymond
Oundle and the English public school.
1. England. Boys public schools, to 1988
I. Title
373.2'22'0942

ISBN 0 905743 56 3

Photographic Acknowledgements
Front Jacket: Robert Rathbone
Back Jacket: Dr James Shapiro

Oundle School supplied many of the photographs
in this book. Reproduced from W G Walker A
History of the Oundle Schools (privately printed,
1956) are those on pp43, 55, 65, 72, 80, 87.

The publishers gratefully acknowledge permission
to reproduce photographs from Bedford School
(pp27, 113); Charterhouse, Brian Souter (p121);
the Provost and Fellows of Eton College (p.25);
Harrow School Archives (p30); Repton School
(p120); the Rotary Club of Oundle/Terry
Hodgkins (pp84, 101, 103); Rugby School (p28);
Shrewsbury School (p31); Uppingham School
(p33); the Warden and Scholars of Winchester
College/E F Sollars (p24); Woodmanstowe,
Surrey (p94).

Other photographs were supplied by: Barclays
Bank plc (p162); Mrs E Berridge (p36); James
Berry (p26(2)); John Catt (p95); Peter Flower
(p95(2)); Michael Fraser (p20); The Grocers'
Company (p44); Jonathan Lee (p96); Jonathan
Leech, The Wildfowl Trust, Slimbridge (p7);
Robert Rathbone (pp19(2), 36, 57, 93, 94(2)); Dr
James Shapiro (pp43, 100, 106, 108, 145, 155);
Derrick Smith, Finedon, Northants (p10).

The publishers are also grateful to Toby Liberman
and Roger Page for help in the preparation of the
map on p171; John Western for the drawing of
Eton College School Yard.

**Extract from *Life's Rich Pageant* by permission
of Hamish Hamilton Ltd.,
© Arthur Marshall, 1982.**

CONTENTS

Dedicated Affectionately
to
Michael and Anne Mills

ACKNOWLEDGEMENTS

David and Toni McMurray, who having sportingly taken the risk of asking a relative outsider like myself to write the book, went out of their way to make me feel even more part of the community than when I was *in statu pupillari*; Colin Cheshire, who as Bursar gave me red carpet treatment; Christiane Freebairn, who organised my research so enthusiastically and efficiently that she really should be called the 'project director', and with her husband Roger Freebairn – poet, literary critic and English master – scrutinized the text with a sharp but benevolent eye;

Alan Rayden, Second Master; Dennis Ford, Librarian; Peter Roberts, Head of the English Department; Alan Midgley, Head of the History Department; Clive Jacques, Rolf Barber, John Matthews, Phillip Swingler, Geoffrey Tristram, David Dew, Richard Mather, Alice Thomas, Jeremy Firth, Robin Veit, Tony Lewin, Richard Andrews, Michael Aubrey, Dick Oldfield and Alan Stuart of The Falcon, Fotheringhay – all of whom most generously offered their specialised knowledge and in some cases read parts of the text; David Richardson, Headmaster of the Laxton School; Pat Ogden, first Headmistress of the Laxton Junior School; Graham Wood, and Kim Morrison who kindly provided material for the Appendix; Roger Eames, Public Relations Officer, who along with my nephew Peter Flower arranged for the illustrations;

Among Old Oundelians, my contemporaries Dick and Gully Wilson and Basil Kenworthy; the late Arthur Marshall, David Newbigging, Lord Hemingford, Frank Spragg, all those who supplied additional material and also Hilary Wharton at the OO office; Among the Governors of the Grocers' Company: W.P. Martineau, Paul Massey, Sir Clive Bossom, Elliott Viney, and Crispin Gascoigne, the present Chairman of the Oundle Committee; Among former headmasters of Oundle: the late Graham Stainforth, Dick Knight, and Dr Barry Trapnell; Archie Nicholson, David Chapman, Anthony Compton Burnett, Mrs Eric Anderson, David Broughton, Jack Cory, and Tom Stacey, the Publisher, for advice about Eton; my cousin David Gaunt, his wife Rose, and Douglas Wilson concerning Harrow; David Warwick concerning Sedbergh; Michael Wynn Jones and John Turner concerning Lancing; Sir Donald Hawley and Peter Batty concerning Radley; the late Bryan Matthews concerning Uppingham; also the Editor of the *Public Schools Year Book*, Jock Burnet.

Last, but certainly not least, my old friend and form mate, Michael Mills, who with his wife Anne originated the whole idea – and to whom, with enormous pleasure, I dedicate this book.

RF
1989

FOREWORD

I T IS A GREAT PLEASURE to be invited to write a Foreword to this excellent book about my old school, which I remember best for introducing me to the great choral works of Bach and Handel, and for the splendid birdwatching, nocturnal bream fishing and rabbit-catching. It set me on course to become a naturalist for the rest of my life.

Raymond Flower is the most prolific of our OO authors, and with some seventeen historical works under his belt – ranging from Switzerland to Singapore, and from Lloyds of London to Motor Racing – it is appropriate that he should have used his experience to tackle Oundle's story from the wider perspective of the evolution of English Public Schools. Most school histories tend to be parochial, but this one is not. Like Oundle, it looks outwards and examines other trees so as to see the whole wood.

Though the school celebrated its Quincentenary in 1985, it is relatively new compared to some of its rivals; Oundle graduated to public school status only in 1876. In 1892 Sanderson arrived and, as a scientist, created the tradition of constantly moving forward into the future, instead of peering backwards into the past. This, of course, is Oundle's secret weapon.

The story of the school is engrossing, as it involves social history too. And here the author is following in the steps of his former housemaster, W.G.(Willie) Walker, who wrote a history of the Oundle Schools some forty years ago. It was privately printed by the Grocers' Company for the Oundelian community. This new history brings the story up to date, and is aimed at a much wider audience. It is vividly written, with a sense of perspective and a gift for anecdote and drama. It is entertaining as well as informative. I wish it every success.

Sir Peter Scott CH CBE DSC FRS
Slimbridge
January 1989

7

PROLOGUE
'THIS LITTLE MARKET TOWN'

PUBLIC SCHOOLS are Britain's most conspicuous contribution to education. You may love them or hate them; you may regard them with mingled sensations of admiration, dislike, pride, envy, or even pity; but you cannot ignore them. So when the Headmaster, David McMurray, and the Governors of Oundle paid me the compliment of suggesting that I should write an up-to-date history of my old school, I resolved to extend the brief. I had in mind an altogether wider concept, in which the story of Oundle would serve to illustrate the evolution of public schools as a whole – a case-history, if you like. I thought I would put Oundle at the centre of the stage, surrounded by its traditional friends and rivals – Bedford, Uppingham, Rugby, Shrewsbury and the rest – and play the history of one against the other, so to speak, while examining, in general terms, the realities of these emblematic establishments from their origins until today.

The story of Oundle begins with the legacy of the Wyatts, who endowed the local chantry school in 1485 – the dynastic year that compilers of examination papers usually take as the dividing line between medieval and modern history.

Although the school was mentioned in the thirteenth century (and even earlier), the Wyatts gave it an economic boost, three-quarters of a century before Sir William Laxton re-endowed it on his death-bed. It could even be argued, as some do, that the original benefactor was Bishop Wilfred in the seventh century.

But for the sake of drama let us begin by visiting Oundle in that significant winter of 1586 (at the time that Kit Marlowe was writing *Tamburlaine the Great* and Shakespeare was probably still a young country schoolmaster) when this little market town suddenly found itself involved in one of the most dramatic episodes in British history. After all, what other places can have seen a monarch, embodying in her person the queen-regnant of Scotland, queen-dowager of France, and queen-claimant of England, being tried and beheaded practically on their doorstep?

Many Catholics regarded Mary as their legitimate queen, and that was the problem. It was also the reason why Mary had been brought to Fotheringhay. Then known as the Eight Hundreds of Oundle, the northern part of Northamptonshire was a Puritan stronghold, and therefore safe country in which to hold her trial. Burghley himself had his seat at Stamford; Sir Walter Mildmay, Elizabeth's Chancellor of the Exchequer, whose brother-in-law Walsingham was in charge of state security, had properties at Apethorpe and Oundle. Together with the Ishams of Lamport, the Montagues of Boughton and other Puritan gentry, the government had sufficient influence in the neighbourhood to prevent the Catholics from stirring up trouble.

But the authorities were taking no chances. Some two thousand troops had been quartered around Fotheringhay Castle when the thirty-four peers who were to conduct the trial arrived with their retinues; Oundle was all bustle and hubbub as the commissioners clattered through, and army quartermasters foraged for supplies and watered the horses.

The interrogation took place in the Great Hall of the Castle. A barrier had been erected, enabling spectators – local people and the servants of the commissioners – to crowd into the back of the chamber. Having heard so much about the legendary Scottish queen, they were eager to see for themselves whether she was really a baleful dragon, or simply a captive princess. Just as Oundelians were curious to see her, so Mary may have welcomed the chance to catch a glimpse of them – practically the only contact she was ever to have with ordinary English folk. William Pamphlon, Laxton School's Puritan Master, would almost certainly have been there with some of his pupils.

They heard her conduct her own defence. She spoke with dignity and style, emphasising the wrongfulness of her imprisonment, and reiterating the significance of her status as a queen. But, as we know, it was to no avail: for the object of the trial was not so much to establish Mary's guilt as to display the evidence on which the judgement was based. And once the theatricals were completed, her life lay at the mercy of Elizabeth.

As the weeks passed, there were constant rumours of an impending execution. Early in February the news leaked out that Mildmay had refused to allow the executioner to lodge at Apethorpe; word went round that he was hidden somewhere in Oundle, with his axe concealed in a trunk. When Lord Shrewsbury and the Earl of Kent arrived with the Clerk of the Council a couple of days later, it was correctly assumed that they had brought the death warrant with them. Early the following morning hundreds of people made their way to the Castle, where they were entertained with music – including an old tune called 'Jumping Joan', which normally accompanied the burning of witches.

Inside, the Great Hall was hung entirely in black. At one end, near a flickering fire, stood the scaffold on a raised platform surrounded by a guard of halberdiers; and by the block, holding a short-handled axe, were stationed the executioner and his assistant. Both wore black masks.

Mary's only reaction to this grim scene was to raise her crucifix as the procession entered the Hall. Dressed in a black satin gown and a white lace veil which flowed down her back to the ground, she stepped on to the stage with immense dignity. Throughout the reading of the death warrant and subsequent proceedings, her expression never changed. But when she disrobed and knelt by the block, the onlookers noticed how vividly her blood-red petticoat and bodice contrasted with the sombre surroundings.

Botching the job, the executioner had to use the axe as a saw to sever her neck before holding aloft the dead woman's head. A final gruesome touch was provided by the discovery

The tower of St Mary's & All Saints Church, Fotheringhay (right) *rises a few miles beyond the School playing fields. Of Fotheringhay Castle where Mary Queen of Scots was tried and executed, nothing now remains but a single stone.*

of Mary's little pet dog, which had somehow managed to hide in her petticoat.

Once the butchery was completed, the spectators trudged home, vaguely aware, perhaps, that things would never be quite the same again. They could hardly have guessed that Oundle was soon to be involved in two other episodes of historical importance. By this time the town had become a centre of Puritan activities. There would have been nothing remarkable about that, to be sure, had events at Oundle – and their repercussions in London – not cast a cloud on the whole Puritan movement.

Previously the chief non-conformists in the locality had been Catholic recusants, led by Gilbert Hussey, a tenant of Sir Thomas Tresham. But the balance changed when Giles Wigginton, one of the earliest Old Oundelians (he was educated at Laxton School, and became a fellow of Trinity College, Cambridge, in 1577) returned to his native haunts having been deprived of his ministry after a brief but stormy career at Sedbergh. An articulate and mischievous critic of the established Church, Wigginton was suspected of being the author of the notorious Marprelate pamphlets attacking episcopacy, and though no longer licensed to do so, he roved around the countryside preaching. In 1589, for instance, he was invited by Robert Johnson (the founder of Oakham and Uppingham schools) to preach in his parish. Undoubtedly Wigginton's presence in Oundle, and the close proximity of the recusants, encouraged extreme attitudes among the Puritans – though nothing as illusory, one would have thought, as the Hacket affair, in which an illiterate Oundelian was proclaimed as the first English messiah.

William Hacket may have been a crackpot. But he married a well-to-do widow and joined forces with Wigginton ('not only a disciple of Wigginton but a partner in malt-making' says

Cosin, the contemporary chronicler.) And despite his lack of education he became bailiff of Oundle, which enabled him to throw his weight about; he was a great fellow for seizing and burning the gaming tables in alehouses on Sundays. But he was also – and this may have been the secret of his success – a comedian with a remarkable talent for mimicry, never failing to raise a laugh at the expense of his foes (above all the unfortunate vicar, who had found it necessary to admit to a charge of incontinence by one of his parishioners).

Detesting ecclesiastic orders, Hacket came to believe that he had a divine calling to sweep away the whole hierarchy. He refused to attend church, and on one of the few occasions that he did was said to have taken 'the surplice from the desk in the church of Oundle where it did stay, and contemptuously in the time of service laid it under his tail'. Soon he became a leader of the radicals; and helped by Wigginton, with William Pamphlon as his scribe (for he could neither read nor write), he launched out on a public career to popularise religion and establish a fully Presbyterian Church in England. That vastly different Puritan zealot, Sir Walter Mildmay, found this too much to stomach. Hacket was promptly locked up in Northampton gaol.

There he claimed to have been visited by an angel, and to be the reincarnation of John the Baptist. On his release, Hacket then went to London and tried to help the other imprisoned *classis* (that is, radical Puritan) leaders. His supporters hailed him as 'King of Europe'. But their activities became so unbalanced that they played into the Government's hands. Hacket was convicted of treason, and executed in Cheapside, ironically for a riot he had not attended. Stow's *Chronicle* tells the story, but the sad episode of the Oundle Messiah is more often alluded to than understood. If nothing else, it illustrates the tensions that existed then between the aims of the lay and clerical leadership, and echoes the sentiments of many discontented folk. Though Hacket may not have been a key figure in the history of Puritanism, his influence should not be discounted.

Next it was the turn of the Catholics to give vent to their frustrations. Their hopes were pinned on James I, who initially seemed so sympathetic to their faith. Yet when the time came for fulfilling promises and half promises, the monarch failed to live up to his word. Hence the Gunpowder Plot. The idea of blowing up Parliament and King was conceived by a few extremists led by Robert Catesby. But one of the chief accomplices was the Oundle landowner, Francis Tresham. Tales are still told of horsemen galloping up to Lyveden in the dead of night; of sinister confabulations at Stoke Doyle and Pilton. And of course, it was Tresham's letter to his brother-in-law, Lord Mounteagle, warning him to stay clear of Parliament, that gave the show away. Thus Oundle was involved, perhaps more than just peripherally, in the famous conspiracy. (Pilton Manor, which belonged to the Treshams, still has its Guy Fawkes room.)

So what with a queen beheaded, a messiah hanged, a local grandee imprisoned in the Tower (Tresham died before he could be executed like the other conspirators), life must have been quite hectic at Oundle in the early days of Laxton's school. Accusing fingers were

Above An aerial view of Oundle looking to the north-east shows the centre of the town which has remained virtually unchanged since the sixteenth century.

pointed at the Master; while over the High Street, Puritans and recusants metaphorically and sometimes physically – for one could easily see from window to window – glared.

Fotheringhay Castle was destroyed, though not perhaps by Mary's son James, as people like to think; nothing more than a weed-covered mound and one massive stone remain. You can still spot the church spire from Oundle's playing fields; and Tresham's unfinished mansion, the New Lyveden building, stands spooky and roofless, albeit splendidly adorned with sculptured biblical texts, on a hill beyond the golf course.

But the nucleus of Oundle remains very much as it was in the sixteenth century. A survey made in 1565 shows the High Street (now West Street, Market Place and North Street) winding though the town just as it does today. Many of the buildings can still be identified:

12

for instance Sir Walter Mildmay's abode, built in 1495 and now sumptuously, if untidily, inhabited by a retired master. In the centre of the Market Place there was a jumble of buildings known as Butchers' Row, and an octagonal monument called The Butter Cross; the Town Hall came later. But the school stood where part of it still stands, overlooking the graveyard of St Peter's Church, whose splendid decorated spire can be seen from miles away and is the focus of the town. Beyond the Vicarage was a horse-pond, with Merton's horse-market alongside; a pub, the White Hart, occupied part of the site of the present School Cloisters.

Across the street, the Tudor-gothic Great Hall and School House have replaced a row of houses owned by a certain Johes Cooke. Of course the fine seventeenth-century mansions – Cobthorne, Bramston, Laundimer, the Berrystead – had not yet appeared to dignify the skyline. But even then a predecessor to the famous Talbot Inn (built in 1625) was known as the Tabret.

Otherwise, the heart of Oundle has barely changed. Indeed the present architectural marriage of town and gown is subtle, as much to do with space and location as with the buildings themselves. Though the school clearly contributes to the town's economy, its presence is never overpowering. A surprising number of town dwellings have been converted for scholastic use, and you feel that there is hardly a nook and scarcely a cranny that has not somehow been pressed into academic service. New House is one of the oldest of them all (Cromwell is reputed to have stayed there). Laundimer was once Lord Lyveden's town house; Old Dryden was formerly the Dolphin Hotel. Junior boys joining the Berrystead find themselves in a mansion of classic proportions. The Congregational Chapel has been stunningly converted into a theatre; the Bursar's office is in the old almshouses.

Yet only a few steps away are Sanderson's great honey-coloured edifices, the Chapel, the Science block and the Yarrow museum, surrounded by lawns and herbaceous borders; and students emerge from late twentieth-century computer buildings to dispute mathematical theories in venerable classrooms at the top of Georgian stairs.

Reassuring and stimulating is this interplay of tradition and modernity. Above all it serves as a reminder that although Oundle can look back into the past, its sights are set firmly on the future.

I

'THE GILD OF OUR LADY OF OUNDLE'

THE ORIGINS OF OUNDLE are pre-Roman. But the town stands where it has always stood on the edge of the old Forest of Rockingham where the river Nene makes a great loop, some thirteen miles south-west of Peterborough.

It is one of the most agreeable small towns in England, and one of the oldest: the very name is so ancient that experts have given up trying to discover its derivation, though they seem to agree that it survives, like the word Nene, from the Celtic period. The Romans apparently called the place Undulum, and vestiges of their settlement were uncovered down by the river when the modern by-pass was being built a few years ago.

But Oundle is first mentioned in historical records as the place where St Wilfred died in AD 708. His name catches the eye because he was one of the earliest great headmasters. Education being the handmaid of religion, the lineal antecedents of our public schools first appeared with the coming of Christianity. 'Older than the House of Commons, older than the Universities, older than the Lord Mayor, older even than the throne or the nation itself' was the effusive claim made by A.F.Leach, the historian, for St Peter's, York (though King's, Canterbury and Rochester were probably earlier still) and Bishop Wilfred became Master of St Peter's, York after the Council of Whitby in 664, when York was the ecclesiastical capital of England. His friend and biographer, Eddius, tells us that secular princes and noblemen gave him their sons to educate as priests, or if they preferred, soldiers. Wilfred was, it seems, 'lighthearted, wrongheaded, full of genius but defective in judgement. The most elegant man of his day, he was overbearing in argument, but in action he was tolerant and generous'.

When the diocese of York was divided into three, Wilfred became Bishop of Leicester, and founded a monastery at Oundle. Of the Saint's final journey, his biographer wrote: 'Last of all they came to his monastery, where of old he had dedicated a church to St Andrew'. And the Venerable Bede confirms that 'he died in his own monastery which he had in the province of Oundle'. Two centuries later when Athelwold, the Bishop of Winchester, came to restore Medehamstede (that is, Peterborough) he found the old site of the monastery of Oundle and rebuilt it too.

As my old housemaster W.G.Walker remarks in his scholarly history of the Oundle Schools, this excursion into the remote past is not irrelevant. For where St Wilfred founded a monastery he also founded a song school, of which a grammar school was the invariable adjunct. Though this is a premise that cannot be proved, such schools grew up at any place where there was a religious institution; and Oundle was then a town of some consequence, giving its name to that part of Northamptonshire. The Domesday Book mentions the existence of markets at Higham Ferrars, King's Sutton and Oundle (though not at either Northampton or Peterborough) so even if a firm link with St Wilfred's foundation cannot be established, common sense tells us that there would have been a school as well. After all, Canute is said to have instituted *publicas scolas* in such places for 'boys of good promise to be taught grammar'.

Be this as it may, in 1223 a certain John of Peterborough was presented with the living of Oundle, on the understanding that he brushed up his education by attending the local school. This was not such an unusual requirement, for in those days many clerics were virtually illiterate and a vicar of Northampton was made to do the same. But at least it suggests that there was a grammar school at Oundle for the new rector to attend.

Moreover few parishes were without a guild, especially in the religious revival that followed the ravages of the Black Death. A religious guild consisted of men and women who paid annual dues and were expected to make bequests to it in their wills. When sufficient funds had been accumulated, the guild would acquire its own chantry; but the first priority was to maintain a priest to sing masses for the souls of the departed, and whenever possible the guild provided an alms-house for a few old people. This cleric was also expected to assist the parish priest with his normal business, and often to teach boys Grammar – that is, Latin – in a school held either in the church or in an adjoining room.

The Gild of Our Lady of Oundle was founded, or rather refounded, by Robert and Joan Wyatt at the end of the fifteenth century. When he died in 1494, Robert Wyatt left twenty shillings to the guild and six shillings and eightpence to its chapel: four years later John Rawlynse of Warmington left a cow to the wardens. It appears therefore, that the guild had been in existence for some time before Joan Wyatt applied for a licence to refound it in 1499.

In his *Itinerary*, John Leland mentions an inscription on the almshouse door dated 1485. This date is now generally accepted as the earliest evidence of a grammar school in Oundle that is directly in line with the present schools.

On 12 June 1499 Joan Wyatt paid 100 shillings for a licence to refound the guild, which really amounts to a charter of incorporation. She herself became a 'lady of the mantle and the ring', that is, she took the widow's vow of chastity for the rest of her life, and when making her own will in 1506 she appointed the aldermen and brethren of the guild as her executors, one of whom was John Laxton.

Dame Joan appears to have endowed the guild with the ground that is now Bramston House garden and paddock. How much more the guild owed to her bequests is not clear, but by the following year the executors had obtained titles to 32 messuages, 16 acres of arable land, and 10 acres of meadow in Oundle, amounting to a yearly value of ten pounds. From subsequent wills the guild received further gifts, including the site of the Tabret, and

The Guild-house of 1485 as it was in 1841 (right) *in a lithograph by B. Rudge of Bedford.*

later the Talbot Inn. Enjoying one of the highest endowments in the county, the guild was able to appoint five stipendiaries. One of them, a local man named William Ireland, became the Master of the grammar school and remained so for the next forty-seven years, retiring in 1554 at the age of eighty-five.

Indeed he outlasted the guild itself. For after the dissolution of the monasteries Henry VIII ordered that all collegiate foundations, chantries and guilds should be made over to the Crown. Commissions to assess their value were appointed, but although the King died before any action could be taken on their findings, the Act was extended in 1548 to include all the endowed schools in the country. Only cathedral schools along with Winchester, Eton and Magdalen College School – which were regarded as part of the universities with which they were connected – escaped confiscation.

The chantries were taken over because they were considered to be theologically offensive, rather than corrupt or inefficient. But fortunately the Edwardian commissioners had the power to allow some schools which were associated with chantries to continue if they thought it desirable. Oundle was fortunate the two commissioners were Sir Walter Mildmay and Robert Keilway of Rutland, both of whom had local connections. In Northamptonshire they approved the continuation of four schools – those at Rothwell, Blisworth, Towcester, and the 'grammer schole' at Oundle.

Nevertheless the Gild of Our Lady of Oundle was suppressed in 1548, leaving the school without funds. For a year or two old Ireland's salary was paid by the Earl of Bedford, who had become the Lord of the Manor, and the school muddled on. But then, at the nadir of its fortunes, a former pupil came to the rescue. And his endowment was backed by the might of a great London institution.

16

II

SIR WILLIAM LAXTON AND THE
'MISTERY' OF THE GROCERS OF THE CITY OF LONDON

WILLIAM LAXTON was born in Oundle at the end of the fifteenth century, the son of John Laxton who was one of the executors of Joan Wyatt's will. From the age of seven until fourteen he went to the grammar school, where he was one of the first pupils of William Ireland, Guild Priest and first Master. Afterwards he moved to London and became apprenticed to a Grocer – very likely Sir John Rast, whose family came from Peterborough, or Sir Henry Keeble of Apethorpe. Seven years later Laxton was admitted as a freeman of the Grocers' Company and began trading on his own. In all probability he became a merchant, like his father, and made his money from overseas ventures – perhaps taking a share in a ship, which in those days led to sudden ruin or a quick fortune. At any rate he prospered, got his livery, and in 1534 was elected a Junior Warden. Clearly he was regarded as a rising man.

In fact Laxton's career, like that of John Rast (who progressed from Warden of the Grocers' Company to Sheriff and then Mayor of London in 1516), shows that in Henry VIII's England upward mobility was possible for an industrious youngster who conformed to the City's conventions and took his chances when they came. Plenty of lads from the provinces rose from rusticity to high office with the help of their guilds – and ended up as founders of famous schools, as we shall see.

The medieval guilds which played such a key role in the City of London were voluntary associations formed for the mutual aid and protection of their members. They were characterised by a strong spirit of cooperation between guildsmen, complemented by a mixture of worldly and religious ideas (the support of the body allied to the salvation of the soul, you might say).

These guilds came into being soon after the Norman Conquest as a result of the increasing importance of trade. They took their inspiration from France and the Italian *Arte*, for there were plenty of Lombards and Florentines in London at that time. Indeed the *Gilda Mercatoria* were regarded as one of the City's most important privileges, implying that they had the prescriptive right to trade freely in their commodities. Consequently the guild ordinances were designed to protect their members from outside competition, and to impose fees and restrictions upon those who wanted to trade. The ordinances were enforced by Master and Wardens working in conjunction with the aldermen of the City. Every so often the guildsmen held feasts, at which they brought the rules up to date, admitted new members, elected officers, and discussed their affairs.

Originally the Grocers' Company – the Wardens and Commonalty of the Mistery of the Grocers of the City of London, to give its full, sonorous title – was known as the *Gilda Pipariorum*, the Pepperers' Guild, and first appears in the Pipe Roll of 1180 when eighteen London guilds were fined for operating without a royal licence. Their trade was not only in pepper but in spices and condiments. And as all these had to be imported, the profits, but also the risks, were enormous. It was the Pepperers' ships, together with Genoese and Venetian galleys, which brought oriental spices to British ports.

Their guild was naturally concerned with weighing (it kept the King's Beam and nominated the garbler), and *peso grosso* is said to be the origin of the word 'Grossarius', which in English became 'Grocer' (and in French *Grossiste*), just as 'Mistery' derives from the term *ministerium*, meaning service or employment, trade or craft. The Guild of Pepperers disappeared in the reign of Edward III (whose wars with France brought ruin to many merchants, including some of the most powerful Florentine bankers) and was replaced in 1345 by a fraternity known as the 'Grossers'. This society attracted some of the leading City businessmen in London. By the end of the century one hundred and three members wore the Grocers' livery, and fifteen the hood, indicating the start of distinction between the grander merchants and the smaller journeymen retailers. They were a powerful body. But they still had no Hall, and had not yet received a Royal Charter of Incorporation.

In 1426 the Grocers purchased Lord Fitzwalter's property in Old Jewry and began building a Hall on the site. Two years later they obtained their charter. (The Merchant Taylors, Goldsmiths, Mercers and Saddlers already had theirs, and nine other great Misteries followed suit very soon afterwards.) Grocers' Hall, paid for by voluntary subscriptions, was finished on 1 July 1431 in time for the ceremonial opening by the Mayor, City dignatories, and the whole Company of Grocers. Alongside the Hall was a garden extending to the banks of the Walbrook, with an arbour, numerous vines and fig trees, a bowling green, and a tennis court.

This impressive institution, whose members conducted their individual businesses and often served as aldermen or Mayor, was the ladder to William Laxton's success. By 1534 he was a warden of the Grocers' Company; and his civic career began when he became alderman for Aldersgate – a job he took seriously, for his name appears on almost every page of the repertories of the mayoralty courts. Two years later he was elected Upper Master, or Chairman, of the Grocers, and was granted the coat of arms which is still used by Laxton School. Next he was chosen to be one of the two sheriffs of the City of London, and in 1544 came the ultimate step when, on 28 October, he took office as Mayor of London. Laxton was the first holder of that office to wear the historic collar of gold, left to the City by Sir John Alleyn, and which has been worn by all successive Lord Mayors. (He can be seen wearing it in the Chapel window and on the Cloisters' gateway tower at Oundle.)

No events of great interest took place during his mayoralty. However, in addition to the normal charges of this expensive office he was faced with the demand for a large subsidy

VNDELLÆ NATVS LONDINI PARTA LABORE
LAXTONVS POSVIT SENIBVS PVERISQVE LEVAMĒ

ΑΘΛΑ ΔΙΔΑΣΚΟΝΤΟΙΝ ΡΕΝΙΧΡΟΙΣ ΕΝΙΑΥΣΙΑ ΛΑΜΠΡΟΣ
ΜΝΑΣ ΤΡΙΑΚΟΝΤ ΟΚΤΩ ΣΥΝΤΕ ΔΟΜΟΙΣΙΝ ΕΔΩ

אשרי תבותך לבתאים ערמה
לתת לבערים מזמחזרעת
אשרי תחרב אבידנים שבעת
לתת לעביים מלובת ולחם

Sir William Laxton re-endowed the Oundle grammar school in 1556. A Victorian statue (left) stands today above the entrance to the School Cloisters. The 'Inscribed Plate' (above) was placed on the Guild-house in 1593 by William Pamphlon. The inscriptions in Latin, Greek and Hebrew record Laxton's gifts to the town for the school and the almshouse.

from the City to pay for Henry VIII's French war. The King's commissioners assessed the amount each alderman should contribute as a 'benevolence', and one alderman who refused to pay was promptly conscripted as a common soldier. But Laxton paid up immediately, and was rewarded with a knighthood.

A few years previously he had married Joan Luddington, the widow of a not very prosperous grocer who had seven children. Three of these survived: a son named Nicholas, whom Laxton later took on as an apprentice, and two daughters. Laxton never had any children of his own. Beyond the family circle, his friends consisted of city magnates, self-made men like himself such as Sir Thomas White, the future founder of St John's College, Oxford, Sir John Gresham, Sir William Harpur, Sir Richard Dobbs, Sir John Lyon and Lawrence Sheriff, all of whom bought property from the Crown after the Reformation, and subsequently became the founders of the great schools.

Clearly Laxton remained in touch with Oundle, for he left legacies to friends in the town as well as to his numerous kinsfolk in Gretton. And knowing the effect that the confiscation of the chantry would have, he began to make plans to endow a free grammar school, with almshouses attached, to perpetuate his memory in the place he was born. In 1553 he asked Sir John Lyon, who was then Master, if the Grocers would accept some freehold property in London and maintain the school from the income.

Sir John was opposed to taking on such a responsibility (though twenty years later he himself endowed Harrow). However, Laxton persisted, and in 1555, when Richard Grafton was one of the wardens, the Company appointed a committee to study the matter. At first they turned it down; and it was only the following year, when Laxton was on his deathbed, that a delegation came to indicate their willingness to accept. According to Grafton, Laxton said he was too ill to be troubled with such a matter at that time. Apparently it was Thomas

Sir WILLIAM LAXTON, a native of this place, grocer in LONDON, and Lord-mayor in the year 1544. died in 1556. He left estates for the Endowment of this grammer School and this Hospital. both which Establishments. He placed under the Superintendance of the grocers company. LONDON. JL.

Wanton, the husband of Sir William's niece (and heir-in-law, since he had founded no family) who persuaded him to make the necessary arrangements – which was ironic in view of the litigation that followed. As Laxton's will had already been signed, sealed and witnessed a couple of days previously, the dying man was advised to add a codicil, which he approved in the presence of his wife and Nicholas Luddington, though he did not actually sign it. Two days later he was dead.

The intent of the codicil was clear: the Grocers would act as governors of the re-endowed school; salaries would be paid to the Master and Usher as well as seven Bedemen; a building which Laxton knew was available would be acquired. To finance the endowment and bring in the necessary income of thirty-eight pounds a year, certain London properties would be made over to the Company.

As a Grocer, Laxton knew that no better governing body could be found than his own company. But he felt that such service should be rewarded. So he did not intend that the whole income from these estates should be devoted to maintaining the school and the almshouses. He wanted the Company to receive any surplus revenue as compensation for their trouble. This was to cause problems later on.

However, an immediate complication was that the Wantons contested the will, not wishing to risk any of their presumptive inheritance. It took seventeen years to sort out the legal entanglements. In the meantime Lady Laxton bought the guild-hall and the priest's house, and herself kept the school in funds.

When the first Master, William Ireland retired at the age of eighty-five, he was replaced by a more impressive figure. A fellow of Jesus College, Cambridge, John Sadler was also one of the original fellows of Trinity College. He seems to have been brought to Oundle by the Earl of Bedford, who as Lord of the Manor, was understandably concerned about the future

The late seventeenth-century inscription (opposite) was re-discovered in 1989. The initials 'J.L.' are those of John Lewis, an 'overseer' elected by the Grocers' Company in 1683. Laxton's bequest to Oundle also included provision for seven bedesmen. They had seven shillings weekly, a Sunday dinner, and wore distinctive dress (seen left with their dame in 1914).

of the school. During his time at Oundle, Sadler made a translation of *De Re Militari* by Vegetius (which secured him a place in the *Dictionary of National Biography*.) His book is dedicated to the Earl, expressing gratitude for the annuity which enabled him to exercise his trade, as he puts it, and this suggests that Bedford had been paying part of his salary. He also received the statutory stipend of five pounds six shillings and eightpence from Lady Laxton until the Exchequer resumed payment on the accession of Queen Elizabeth in 1558.

Though there were forty-eight pupils, Sadler appears to have run the school singlehanded in the guild-hall until he was appointed rector of Sudborough in 1568. He may have provided a curate to run his parish, yet it seems more likely that he retained a young Oundle man to carry on his work at the school. One of the stories about Hacket is that he bit off this poor fellow's nose in a quarrel. (The local surgeon, who was present, asked for the nose in the hope of sticking it back. But – says our chronicler – the 'cannibal varlet not only utterly refused to part with it, but held it up triumphantly, and showed it with great vaunterie and glory to all that would behold it, and after did in most spiteful and divelish outrage eat it up'.)

At all events John Sadler remained long enough at Oundle to see the old guild school through until it was re-endowed. In 1573 the legal battle with the Wantons was finally settled, and the Grocers' Company was able to carry out Laxton's wishes. At this point Sadler retired to his rectory and another fellow of Trinity College, Cambridge became Master at Oundle.

Chosen on Sir Walter Mildmay's recommendation, the new candidate was Ralph Wilkinson, Doctor of Physic – Oundle's first 'science headmaster'. But Wilkinson was a good classical scholar as well. His commonplace book, which can be seen in the British Museum, is full of quotations from Euripides and Livy written in a stylish hand. In any case he was assisted by an usher, so the four dozen boys continued to be taught Latin rather than Physics.

Mildmay also made sure that the buildings were shipshape. The guild-house and the master's dwelling were restored. After seven years in office Wilkinson resigned to resume his medical career. His successor was another Trinity man, the 'Oundle Messiah's' friend, William Pamphlon.

III

ANCIENT FOUNDATIONS

HAVING FOLLOWED the evolution of Oundle to the point where it was firmly established as a free grammar school, we should now take a look at the development of some other educational establishments. For it is surprising how many ancient foundations ran a similar, if not parallel, course.

Laxton's colleagues in the City were responsible for several of the new foundations. Sir William Harpur, who preceded him as Mayor, founded Bedford in 1552. Sir John Gresham of the Fishmongers' Company, with whom Laxton served as alderman for many years, established Gresham's Holt in 1554. Tonbridge was endowed in 1562 by Sir Andrew Judde, Warden of the Skinners' Company, whose name frequently appears alongside those of Laxton and Gresham in the repertories of the Mayor's court. Sir John Lyon was Master of the Grocers' Company in 1553; he secured the charter for Harrow in 1571, and subsequently endowed the school. Lawrence Sheriff occupied the same post in 1566, and founded Rugby the following year.

These Tudor magnates shared similar characteristics. They were self-made men who came to London to make their fortunes; they achieved high office through being members of a great Livery Company – often the Grocers. They used their money to buy up church or chantry land seized by the Crown, and with this they endowed a school in the places where they were born and brought up. Usually they provided for the old as well as the young by founding almshouses.

Many of the founders were childless, and perhaps for this reason hoped to perpetuate their names and their achievements. But like the monarch herself, they could not bear to contemplate their mortal end. Thus many of the endowments were last minute affairs – codicils to wills tucked under the death-bed blankets. Not surprisingly, this resulted in lawsuits, even before the schools were built.

But of course many were re-foundations. As early as the thirteenth century elementary schools were to be found scattered all over the country, and most market towns supported establishments of a higher type known as grammar schools, in which boys were taught to speak, read and write Latin. Parents were anxious to send their sons to them, but though education was free there were difficulties for the poor. In those days every man who did not own a certain quantity of land was compelled to bring his sons up to his own occupation, and failure to do so meant the boy was not being prepared for his appointed life's work. Numerous instances are recorded of parents being fined for sending their children to school.

However, the Black Death, which ravaged the country for forty years and killed about a third of the population, had important repercussions. It led to the Statute of Labourers (1351), one clause of which stated that 'any man whatever his condition, might send his son to any school he liked to learn grammar' and to the Peasants' Revolt (1381).

This was a milestone in educational history. After 1409 those who went to school were more likely to be the offspring of poorer parents, for whom even an elementary knowledge of Latin could be crucial in determining their place in society. William of Wykeham, the immensely rich bishop of Winchester, and Chancellor of England anticipated such a

development when he founded Winchester College in 1382[1]. It was a new departure: a school with ten Fellows and seventy pupils who were all to be poor local boys. These would be educated and put up free; and while first priority was given (well, why not?) to the founder's kin, the others were to be drawn from the local diocese or from parishes where the College owned property. Provision was also made for accepting ten sons of noblemen and 'other worthy persons', but only as fee-paying boarders. Henry VI founded Eton in 1440 on much the same basis. Again there were to be seventy poor scholars from the College's estates, along with thirteen others who paid their way by doing domestic work. In addition, twenty-five sons of the aristocracy could be admitted against the payment of fees.

Winchester was founded in 1382 by William of Sykeham, Bishop of Winchester and Chancellor of England. The Middle Gate and Chamber Court (opposite) *date from 1390. Eton was founded in 1440 by Henry VI. School Yard is seen left.*

Yet as it turned out, few of the medieval élite were educated at Winchester or Eton. To the aristocracy and landed gentry education meant equipping them for their own way of life. Their scions were normally trained in a large baronial household, or preferably a royal one, where they served as pages, performing menial tasks such as waiting at table. As members of their host's family they learnt etiquette and deportment, the rules of precedence and courtly conversation. They were taught how to ride, joust, hunt, hawk, the wearing of armour and military skills. Such matters were considered more important than acquiring academic knowledge. Of course there were exceptions. Bishop Alcock, who tutored Edward IV's son at Ludlow Castle (and who also founded Jesus College, Cambridge) insisted that

---

[1]The College, like its sister foundation, New College, Oxford, was to consist of a Warden, seventy 'poor indigent scholars', ten priest fellows, three priest chaplains, three clerks and sixteen choristers. These numbers were symbolic: the Warden and fellows represented the Apostles (minus Judas); the masters and scholars represented the disciples (72 in number according to the Vulgate); the chaplains and the clerks corresponded to the deacons (minus the apostate Nicholas) and the sixteen choristers corresponded to the four major and twelve minor prophets.

the Prince of Wales should be instructed 'in grammar, music and other cunning, and exercises of humanity'.

A few members of the aristocracy – usually younger sons who were expected to supplement their patrimony by a career in government or the Law – were sent to grammar schools. But more often they went to the Inns of Court, where in addition to being taught the airs and graces of a nobleman they were trained in professional skills. By the beginning of the sixteenth century there were over 300 students at the Inns; the list of Queen Elizabeth's Privy Council in the middle of her reign shows that whereas none of them went to either Winchester or Eton, about half were at Oxford or Cambridge, and nearly all passed through the Inns of Court.

If the antecedents of today's public schools can be traced back to the medieval system of baronial households, cathedral chantries, and the Inns quite as much as to the great colleges, the old grammar schools also played their part in the genesis. But their development was encouraged by trade.

The shortage of labour following the Black Death meant that large areas were turned to pasture, and as the sheep population increased so did the production of wool. The surplus was exported, chiefly to Flanders. One of the Oundle wool merchants had an office in Calais. (When his wife wrote to confirm that some cartloads of wool were on their way, he replied complaining about the French food, and said he missed the fat venison and good wine at home.)

To deal with this foreign trade it was necessary to train clerks at home and representatives for abroad; and Latin being the only universally understood language, the wool merchants began to take an interest in grammar schools. Thus a free school was endowed at Oswestry by David Holbeach, a lawyer, at the beginning of the fifteenth century, while the first to be founded by a London merchant, William Sennake of the Grocers' Company, was Sevenoaks in 1432. (Significantly, Sennake laid down that the Master was not to be in holy orders.) A spate of schools followed, some endowed by bishops, but mostly by businessmen: schools at Stockport, Macclesfield, Cromer and Week St Mary were all created as chantries by ex-Mayors of London at the turn of the sixteenth century. And another wave of new foundations followed the dissolution of the chantries. Convinced that poverty bred ignorance and popery, Protestant merchants were more generous than ever. In the century that followed, 109 endowed schools and 49 unendowed schools were founded or refinanced by Londoners alone.

These schools took boys between the ages of six and eight, and aimed to teach their pupils enough Latin to enter Oxford or Cambridge at sixteen, or even earlier. Yet only a few of their scholars actually went to the universities, just as only a few of the foundations grew into famous public schools. We are concerned with those that did, and which in one way or another are of special interest to Oundle. So let us take a quick glance at some of them.

Bedford, for instance – a great rugger and cricket rival. Though Bedford is usually

Bedford was founded in Edward VI's reign (1547-1553). The Old School Buildings are seen above.
It became a sporting rival to Oundle in the twentieth century.

considered to have been founded in Edward VI's reign, it is, like Oundle, almost certainly a monastic and pre-Conquest foundation. There is reference to the school in a document from the reign of Henry II, when the borough received it first charter (with the privilege to form a merchant guild, levy tolls, and create freemen, which in due course was to cause so much trouble). At the dissolution of the monasteries, the school was handed over to the Mayor and Commonality. Subsequently Edward VI's commissioners – Mildmay and Keilway – gave it a licence to continue. So when Sir William Harpur, a native of Bedford, endowed his old school with land to the north of Holborn (which is still administered by the Harpur Trust) he was, like his friend Laxton, sponsoring an institution that had existed for centuries.

In fact, it must have continued much the same as before, although a few boarders were admitted during the following century. But Bedford remained, as it is today, predominantly a day school. In the eighteenth century, like so many others, it went through a period of decline. In 1769 the original foundation was split into two, Bedford Grammar continuing with a classical curriculum whereas Bedford Modern, as the name implies, taught mathematics and more practical subjects. Consequently, by the end of the century there were only 18 pupils in the original grammar school. However, when Dr Brereton became headmaster in 1811, he put the place back on its feet, providing sounder tuition and taking boarders into his own house. For all this Bedford remained small, and its emergence as a great public school dates from the arrival of Phillpots in 1875. During his twenty-eight years as Headmaster pupil numbers rose to over eight hundred. Many of the boys were sent by parents stationed overseas, and so rapid was the expansion that the school had twice to move into new premises. Indeed, the old grammar school building became the Town Hall. By then there was a good deal of rivalry between the two sister schools, which added to the fun.

Rugby was younger, but achieved fame earlier. Lawrence Sheriff, who witnessed Laxton's will and supplied Elizabeth I with groceries, seems to have founded it from scratch. (Incidentally, apart from being Master of the Grocers' Company, Sheriff was well known for his heretical opinions. We are told that his neighbour, Farrer, hoped to see him 'hop headless, or frying among the faggots'. In return Sheriff, who supported the Reformation, complained to the Bishop of London that Farrer made fun of Elizabeth, whom he called a "Jill".

Be this as it may, Sheriff's will, dated 22 July 1567, endowed his new school with a mansion in the town and the parsonage of Brownsover. However, five weeks later, when literally on the point of death, he added a codicil to include a third of his estate in Middlesex, and these eight acres became the basis of the school's subsequent prosperity.

Even so Rugby's prosperity was not immediately apparent. For one thing the endowment only brought in twenty-five pounds at first. In his will, Sheriff directed that the Trust was to be administered by two of his friends, George Harrison and Bernard Fields, and their heirs 'for ever'. The two men built a school house by the master's residence opposite the

Rugby, seen right in an 1816 drawing by Ackerman, was founded in 1567 by Lawrence Sheriff, who witnessed Sir William Laxton's will and was also Master of the Grocers' Company.

parish church and installed Edward Rolston as first Master in 1574. But after they died things began to go wrong. Tenants ceased payments and there was a period of continuous litigation, during which time Rugby vegetated. A later master, Rafael Pearce, saw his salary diminish to almost nothing. When he died in 1651, the school must have been closed for a period since his successor, Peter Whitehead, was not appointed until some months later.

Whitehead is said to have been 'very diligent and painfull in the schoole' and no doubt he improved matters. But it was under Henry Holyoake, the first of its notable masters, that Rugby finally began to thrive. Holyoake had been chaplain of Magdalen College, Oxford, before being expelled with other Protestant fellows by James II. On his arrival in 1687 he began to concentrate on taking in boarders, hoping no doubt to augment his own income. However, he did so with such success that the numbers rose quickly to just under a hundred. As its reputation spread, Rugby began to attract not only sons of the local gentry, but pupils from as far afield as Cheshire, Somerset and Kent. Moreover by 1750 the value of the Trust had increased dramatically, enabling the trustees to extend the buildings. They bought the Manor House and built a new school, very much like the old one, alongside it.

All the same there was a decline under the next Master, and in 1778 Stanley Burrough handed over only 52 boys to his successor, Thomas James, the first to be called a 'headmaster'. In his own words James brought Cambridge scholarship and Eton methods, declaring that he ruled by 'the principles of justice rather than by the terror of the rod', though this did not prevent him from spending two guineas a year (about a fifth of a working man's wages) on canes and birches.

Reorganising the curriculum with an efficiency that paved the way for Arnold, James introduced the tutorial system along with such innovations as Dames' houses, praeposters and fagging, which became the cherished trappings of every Victorian public school. But he was also faced with two schoolboy rebellions, one of which was led by the future General Sir Willoughby Cotton, who later put down the 'slaves rebellion' in Jamaica. Amongst James' notable pupils were Samuel Butler, who became Shrewsbury's great headmaster; Charles Apperley, the celebrated 'Nimrod' of *The Gentleman's Magazine*; and Walter Savage Landor (who was expelled for writing some scurrilous verses in the headmaster's album).

In James' time new classrooms were built with dormitories above them for boarders, though it was left to his successors to complete what are now known as the 'Old Buildings'. Thus half a century before Arnold's arrival Rugby became more than just a grammar school. With 380 boys, it joined the élite few that Dr Johnson called the 'great' schools.

Harrow reached this status much earlier. Of all the schools created by Laxton's friends, Harrow benefited most from the founder's statutes. Sir John Lyon gave a great deal of thought to the wording of his endowment. But though his intention was to provide education for thirty poor boys in the parish, he included a stipulation that fee-paying pupils could be admitted from any part of the country. Consequently the school, so conveniently situated ten miles from London on the hill where St Anselm had consecrated the Church

of St Mary, soon attracted rich boarders, and its masters quickly saw the advantages of admitting pupils who paid rather than those who did not.

Hide, who was headmaster from 1628 to 1661, opened up a boarding house and initiated the employment of Dames – that is, landladies who could teach the younger boys to read in their houses. A hundred years later Dr Robert Sumner went a step further by allowing the Dames to open boarding houses within the school, and these lasted well into the nineteenth century. Already in Sumner's time there were complaints that Harrow had become unsuitable for day boys because of the scorn and bullying they had to endure from wealthy boarders with extravagant habits. In 1809 the matter was taken to the Court of Chancery, which decided that under the terms of Lyon's will the school authorities were entitled to take in as many boarders as they could accommodate. But long before then Harrow had shed any semblance of being a free grammar school.

In the eighteenth century it became a very rowdy place. Partly this was a reflection of an age that, for all its veneer of social grace and intellectual enlightenment, was nevertheless violent. Fighting was regarded as a test of social acceptability – an approved form of sport at a time when organised games were unknown. Necessity made a virtue of *laissez-faire*; there were never enough masters to keep order outside the classroom, and boys were therefore left to their own devices. So long as they kept within bounds they were free to do as they liked. Discipline was enforced by the seniors, on the theory that the only way to govern boys was to train them to govern themselves. But of course it meant that the responsibility for curbing such pursuits as drinking, gambling, and sex fell on the very boys who were usually the chief offenders.

Puerile power led to three revolts, two of which were provoked by the appointment of a

Harrow was founded in 1571 by Sir John Lyon. The 'form room' of the School dates from 1615, seen opposite *in a photograph of 1875. It was the tradition for boys to carve their names on the oak panels when they left – among them Robert Peel and Anthony Trollope*

Shrewsbury (seen Left *in 1870) was given a charter in 1552 by Edward VI. By 1586 it had become, according to Camden, 'the largest school in all England'.*

headmaster the lads did not like. When Benjamin Heath was chosen instead of the popular usher, Dr Parr, they went on such a rampage that the governor's coach was smashed to pieces. Another revolt occurred on the retirement of Dr Drury, who was so popular that when he left the boys unhorsed his carriage and drew it themselves up the hill. They wanted his son Mark as headmaster and when H.M. Butler was appointed, the monitors, led by Byron, staged a rebellion. Byron is said to have carried a loaded pistol to shoot the new headmaster, and to have toyed with the idea of blowing up the school. (Before leaving for Greece the poet apologised to his old master, and they parted good friends.)

But oddly enough the most serious riot took place when Butler confiscated the canes that were the symbols of the monitors' authority. For instead of rejoicing, the rest of the school sided with the monitors (which gives cause for thought). There was a strike lasting four days, during which the London road was blockaded. After order had been restored, Butler expelled seven of the monitors, and was congratulated by George III.

Up in Shropshire, Shrewsbury also became fashionable quite early on. Again we find that the original grammar school was among the 259 which disappeared as a result of the Reformation, but in this case the Charter for a new foundation was given by the Edwardian commissioners in 1551 as a result of petitions from the local people. Thomas Ashton, who was appointed ten years later, is regarded as having been the first headmaster, if not the actual founder. For not only did he canvass for endowments and compile the statutes by which the school was governed for the next two centuries, but he took in nearly eight hundred boys during the first six years of his mastership. Of these 277 were day-boys; the other 523 who came from other parts of the country, lodged in private houses, and paid fees.

Since many were the children of leading families in Shropshire and the neighbouring counties, the school got off to a vigorous start – 'the best filled in all England' says Camden, a former headmaster of Westminster. During the first few years there were never less than four hundred boys *in statu pupillari*, a figure that neither Westminster nor Eton reached until much later.

A timber-framed building was bought in the centre of Shrewsbury, where Ashton had three assistants to help him teach. In Camden's opinion he was 'a right good man', as much at home in Elizabeth's court as with his fellow townsmen. What struck people most was his love of drama. Ashton encouraged acting, and during his time Shrewsbury became known for its Whitsuntide plays, which were expanded into full-scale pageants by his second master and successor, Thomas Laurence. The boys were encouraged to practise archery, jumping, wrestling and running. They were also allowed to play chess and gamble for limited stakes, a penny a game or fourpence a match, though all other betting 'openlie or covertlie' was severely punished.

These aristocratic pastimes created a tradition of unusual sports. Later on the runs were organised as a hunt. The captain, known as the huntsman, and senior 'whips' carried hunting crops and horns; the other runners were the hounds. At the end of the Easter term the hunt was brought to an end with junior and senior steeplechases, with printed race-cards giving the names of the 'horses' and 'owners' – the latter being boys who helped the runners to train, and encouraged them along the last stretch to the winning post.

Unfortunately much of the early éclat was lost during John Meighton's long mastership of over fifty years. But it is of interest to Oundelians to know that his successor, Thomas Challoner, had been the defeated candidate when Johnson was chosen as Master of Oundle in 1637.

Challoner was appointed headmaster of Shrewsbury in the year that Hampton made his stand against ship money; he was expelled by Cromwell and came back with Charles II. Yet despite varying fortunes he managed to revive the school from the atrophy it suffered from under Meighton and during the Commonwealth (when plague caused the place to be closed for some months). One wonders what he might have done at Oundle had he been given the chance; though it must be said that after his death Shrewsbury began to sink as rapidly as Oundle did. When Samuel Butler took over in 1798 there were only eighteen boys in the school.

Under Butler, Shrewsbury built up a formidable reputation for classical scholarship. Once his teaching bore fruit, Salopians won more university distinctions than any other school in the country (and Kennedy's *Latin Primer*, written by a succeeding headmaster, became the staple diet for small boys). In 1882 the school moved from the old buildings in town to a magnificent new site overlooking the river Severn and became, among other things, a great name in rowing circles.

That other famous nursery for sportsmen, Uppingham, was founded by the Rev. Robert Johnson in 1584. Johnson was rector of North Uppingham, and a Puritan with strong radical

Uppingham's School Room (left), which dates from 1584, was provided by Archdeacon Robert Johnson. It is now the Art School.

connections, an anomaly that did not prevent him from being appointed Archdeacon of Leicester – for great Rutland landowners like the Cecils and the Harringtons were covertly promoting Puritanism as a bulwark against papism. Oakham was already a Puritan centre, and, as we said, Johnson let Giles Wigginton, the Oundle radical, preach in his parish.

Today we would describe Johnson as a scholar who combined an interest in education with a social conscience. Having the gift to 'surprise a miser into charity' he successfully collected subscriptions to endow schools at Oakham and Uppingham. Intended to teach grammar freely to the local boys and provide exhibitions to the universities, the twin foundations had Puritan trustees and were governed by their statutes for almost three hundred years. Uppingham and Oakham subsisted uneventfully as country grammar schools, with occasional ups and downs caused by rivalry between each other.

What brought Uppingham to life was the arrival of Edward Thring in 1853, though the generally accepted myth that Thring singlehandedly turned Uppingham into a great public school is not entirely fair. In small ways the process had begun under his immediate predecessor, Henry Holden, who introduced the praeposter system, founded the school library, started the school magazine, and improved the accommodation for boarders.

Indeed Uppingham shares many similarities with the story of Oundle: endowment by an Elizabethan worthy followed by centuries of rural stasis, broken by the arrival of a brilliant headmaster who, working on ground that had been prepared by a predecessor, gave the school its distinctive character and brought it to eminence. This was so often the pattern – one thinks of James and Arnold at Rugby, Holden and Thring at Uppingham, Reade and Sanderson at Oundle. But if the parallels are striking, the substance varies; and at this point we must return to Oundle to look at its development in greater detail.

IV

LONG HOURS AT HARD BENCHES

I N ELIZABETHAN TIMES social and political pressures influenced education. Previously, as we know, most formal schooling had been associated with the Catholic Church, and was geared to train priests rather than teach ordinary pupils. Moreover little value was attached to classical education. Early in the sixteenth century Sir Thomas Elyot complained about those who 'without shame dare affirm that to a gentleman it is a notable reproach to be well learned and to be called a great clerk'. The general opinion was expressed by a landowner who declared that he would rather his son 'should hang than be learned'.

However the Reformation changed people's views and when it became evident that schools had a vital role to play in the struggle to keep England Protestant, Queen Elizabeth's officers of state began to take a closer interest in education.

During a dinner at Windsor Castle in December 1563, Cecil, Mildmay and Sackville were among those who discussed the news that some schoolboys had recently run away from Eton. 'Young children were sooner allured by love than driven by beating to attain good learning', observed Roger Ascham, the Queen's former tutor. He expressed his ideas with such conviction that Sackville urged him to write a book.

Appropriately Ascham's *The Scholemaster* begins with this dinner at Windsor:

I have strange news brought me, saith Mr Secretary, this morning, that divers scholars of Eton be run away from the school for fear of beating. Whereupon Mr Secretary (Cecil) took occasion to wish that some more discretion were in many schoolmasters in using correction than commonly there is; who many times punish rather the weakness of nature than the fault of the scholar; whereby many scholars that might else prove well be driven to hate learning before they know what learning meaneth, and so are made willing to forsake their book and be glad to be put to any other kind of living.

Mr Petre, as one somewhat severe of nature, said plainly that the rod only was the sword that must keep the school in obedience and the scholar in good order. Mr Wotton, a man mild of nature, with soft voice and few words, inclined to Mr Secretary's judgement, and said, in mine opinion the schoolhouse should be in deed, as it is called by name, the house of play and pleasure and not of fear and bondage; and as I do remember, so saith Socrates in one place of Plato.

This incident took place while William Malim was headmaster. His *Consuetudinarium*, written for the information of a Royal Commission which visited Eton in 1561, shows that there was not much play or pleasure at a boarding school in those days.

The boys were woken up at 5 a.m. by a thundering cry of *'surgite!'*. Repeating prayers while dressing, they then made their beds, cleaned the room, and filed down to wash their hands at the pump. At six they had to be in their places in the schoolroom for prayers. From that moment onwards until seven in the evening, with intervals for breakfast at nine, prayers at ten, dinner at eleven, supper at five, and an hour's break in the afternoon, they were engaged in learning Latin or Greek passages by heart, which the Fourth form had to translate, the Fifth to vary, and the top forms to put into verse. After supper they did prep under the supervision of a praeposter (a Seventh-form boy appointed by the headmaster to teach the others) and at eight they went to bed.

And this went on every day of the year, except on religious holidays. The only time they were allowed home was from Ascension Day to Corpus Christi, a period of less than three weeks. No wonder they ran away from such a spartan régime.

If Ascham was all for humanising education, Thomas Becon, a religious reformer, believed that schoolmasters should be enlisted as militant auxiliaries to the 'godly' clergy:

> If the youth of the Christians were thus brought up from their tender years furnished with the armours of the holy scriptures against the damnable opinions of the papists and of such other wicked sectaries as the devil hath raised up in this our time, the Christian commonweal should soon have another face both in doctrine and manners.

It was essential to make sure that schoolmasters adhered to the recently established Anglican Church and did not spread either Catholic or radical Protestant propaganda.

Therefore teachers were required to have episcopal licences. The Canons of 1571 reinforced this control:

> It shall not be lawful for any to teach the Latin tongue or to instruct children, neither openly in the schools neither privately in any man's house, but whom the bishop of that diocese hath allowed and to whom he hath given licence to teach under the seal of his office...
>
> Schoolmasters shall teach no grammar but only that which the Queen's Majesty hath commanded to be read in all schools throughout the whole realm, neither any other Latin catechism than that which was set forth in the year 1570.

In short, education was a politically sensitive issue when William Pamphlon arrived at Oundle in 1583. This was, incidentally, the year Mildmay founded Emmanuel College, Cambridge, which became a Puritan college, and with which Oundle, thanks to Sir Walter, has had close links from the start. In fact, less than a fortnight after Queen Elizabeth granted its charter, Mildmay wrote to the Grocers' Company suggesting that Oundle scholars should be offered two exhibitions every year at Emmanuel.

Like several of the Queen's principal counsellors, Mildmay was a Puritan; and just as Cecil helped his kinsman, Robert Browne (who led the Congregationalist breakaway) so Sir

The Berrystead (above) is one of Oundle's finest seventeenth-century mansions. It was bought by the School in 1911. (Left) A class of c.1932-3 on the steps which, with the front door, have become the House emblem. The author is seated third row from the front, second from the right.

Walter may have had a hand in Pamphlon's appointment.

There is no doubt that he was well fitted for the job. The new master was a skilful linguist, who may even have taught Hebrew in addition to Latin and Greek. It was Pamphlon who placed a brass plate over the guild-house door bearing the school's arms along with a trilingual inscription (which can still be seen in the Laxton School Cloisters). He seems to have conducted the school competently and been liked by the pupils. But unfortunately he was a radical.

Pamphlon must have been delighted to witness the execution of the Catholic Queen of Scots. He may even have encouraged Hacket to organise a watch against papists when Philip II's Armada was sighted in the Channel. It is difficult to say how far he supported the egregious 'Oundle Messiah'. But there is no doubt that he helped Hacket with correspondence which the government regarded as treasonable.

All this was a long time ago, and, sadly, documentation is scarce. But from the records, or lack of them, it seems that the Grocers' Company ignored these radical activities until they realised that Pamphlon was becoming a dangerous liability. In the end, after consultations with Archbishop Whitgift at Lambeth and Lord Burghley at the Queen's court, they put pressure on him to resign.

A pity, because having dismissed one master, they found themselves in the invidious position of having to dismiss the next three. If Pamphlon had to go because of his religious views, his successor turned out to be an incompetent teacher. The next man was a drunkard; and the last, a youngster, committed – in the words of my old housemaster – the unpardonable sin for a schoolmaster.

It was not that the governors were negligent; on the contrary, they did their best to choose the right man. After interviewing a number of candidates, they selected Richard Spencer, an M.A. from Clare Hall, Cambridge, to replace Pamphlon. And at first he appeared to be doing well. Perhaps the Grocers were too busy helping to create the East India Company to follow developments at Oundle too closely. But in 1604 they decided to hold a visitation. The visitors found sixty boys at the school. However, when examined, these pupils turned out to be 'very weak and imperfect, especially in their congruity of Latin'.

Worse still, a number of the parents were dissatisfied. Thomas Tresham of Pilton said his son had spent three years at the school and was a worse scholar when he left than when he had come; a Mr Brooksby complained that in two years his stepson had learnt nothing. Clearly neither the master nor his usher were much good at teaching.

Spencer appealed for mercy: he had a large family and promised to do better if given the chance. So the visitors compromised by approving the appointment of a new usher. When James I passed through Oundle on the way to his new capital the school greeted him in style; and after that it seemed inappropriate to dispense with a schoolmaster who had just enjoyed the favour of a royal visit.

On their next visitation in 1613 the governors were welcomed by a hundred boys and a rather more confident master. But once again the results were disastrous. From the highest to the lowest, reported the examiners, the pupils 'were all very raw, weak, and ignorant scholars'. In vain Spencer presented a list of his boys who had been accepted at the universities. This time he had to go.

He was replaced by Richard Pemberton, a graduate of Trinity College, Cambridge, with Robert Henson, who had just been ordained deacon at Peterborough, as his usher. For the next eighteen months, nothing of interest happened. Then the overseers at Oundle began to complain. They considered both master and usher to be negligent and unsuitable.

So another visitation was ordered. And on this occasion, although more than half the eighty boys were away harvesting, those who were present struck the examiners as 'very well instructed, proving the great pains, care and diligence of the schoolmaster'. They reported that when set a theme to turn into Latin verse, one boy did so well that the wardens gave him a prize. The young versifier was probably Peter Hausted, a playwright and poet who wrote a satire on simony entitled *The Rival Friends*. What's more, both Pemberton and his assistant were described by their neighbours as being sober and honest. Altogether it seemed as though the accusations were unjustified.

Parenthetically, William Lilly, the astrologer, later gave a list of what he read at Oundle under Pemberton: in Latin, *Sententiae Pueriles*, Cato, Corderius, Aesop, Tully's *Offices*, Ovid's *Tristia*, Virgil and Horace; in Greek, Camden's *Greek Grammar*, Theognis, the *Iliad*; and Udall's *Hebrew Grammar*. An impressive catalogue! In his last two years, Lilly says, he could speak Latin just as well as English, and write extempore verses.

The wardens gave a dinner for the masters, the overseers and other local dignitaries, and returned to London satisfied. However, a year or two later there were fresh and more urgent complaints. It was stated that Pemberton, though in orders, had very little regard for religion; he had become slack, and worse still was 'an ordinary haunter and frequenter of alehouses, and other unfitting places . . . to the hurt of his body and scandal to his profession'.

When formally faced with the accusation of being an alcoholic, which he did not deny, Pemberton resigned with a grant to provide for his wife and five children, and once again the governors looked around for a replacement.

Of five applicants, the choice narrowed down to either Samuel Cobb or Anthony Death. Unfortunately Death was selected, probably because his recommendations were stronger. Educated at the Merchant Taylors' School, he had just taken his M.A. at Pembroke Hall, Cambridge, and was twenty-five years old.

Despite his good credentials, Death did not last long. Trouble started almost immediately over the choice of an usher. Next, the Worshipful Company must have been shocked to receive the following letter from the overseers in Oundle:

> Lest your Company should take our silence in ill part we have writ a word or two to let you understand that Mr Death, our schoolmaster, is in trouble at this present being accused to take sundry of his scholars, being the most pretty and amorous boys, to take of them over and over

one alone in to the study at the end of the school, and to send for some of them to his chamber at his lodging . . . Four boys (whereof one of sixteen years of age and another of thirteen or fourteen) have been called before Mr Herenden a Justice of Peace in our town, and being examined have all under their hands affirmed that he used towards them sorry, wanton behaviour. Yea, Mr Death himself hath confessed under his hand some touching of them that might have been spared.

There is five or six more not examined, and truly their parents are loath they should be, lest this business grow to an higher nature and touch upon life: for there are too bad words spread abroad.

As the records were destroyed during the Civil War, the result of Death's trial is not known. But he was promptly sent packing from Oundle. Later he became Master of Carlisle Grammar School, only to be expelled from that ancient establishment at the Restoration, this time for his religious views. (It must be rare, comments Walker, in his *History of the Oundle Schools*, for a headmaster to be dismissed twice, once for being too little a Puritan, and the second time for being too much of one.)

The governors then appointed Samuel Cobb in his place, and at last they struck lucky. The result was astonishing: almost immediately the school took on new life and entered a period of remarkable prosperity. Boys who had been withdrawn from the school returned, and others came from all over the country, even from abroad – indeed one arrived from Elsinore in Denmark. Soon there were over a hundred pupils at Oundle, an impressive number considering that the population of England was only about an eighth of wha it is now. What's more, many boys came from towns which had grammar schools of their own. For about a quarter of a century, from the accession of Charles I until the Civil War, Oundle clearly enjoyed a higher reputation than almost any other comparable school.

This increased prestige shows what an energetic master could do. True, Cobb was assisted by a brilliant young usher, William Dugard, who later became Master of the Merchant Taylors' school, and a noted writer and publisher. (For printing Salmasiuses' *Defensio Regia* he spent a month in Newgate prison before being rescued by Sir James Harrington and restored.)

Dugard's chief contribution at Oundle was to provide a Register of the scholars, which remained in use until 1848. He was a fine penman and the school register, written in Latin, is an imposing document bound in calf. He opened it on 15 September 1626 with a list of 68 boys, grouped in the form order he found them on his arrival. A further 75 entries followed between October 1626 and June 1629, and since the parents' names are mentioned, the register gives a precise indication of the state of the school at that time.[1]

---

[1]The Winchester Long Roll of 1653 is usually considered to be the oldest existing list of any English school, along with the Westminster Roll of 1655, though Shrewsbury has a list of 1562. So Oundle's Roll, if not the oldest, would appear to be older than Winchester's.

From it we know that 29 of the original 68 pupils came from Oundle itself and the other 44 from the neighbourhood or further afield. But over the next ten years the trend changed: an analysis of the 215 names shows that the local boys were outnumbered by more than three to one.

The school attracted a cross-section of English society. From Oundle itself came Cobb's own sons, along with those of the vicar, two lawyers, the veterinary surgeon, three gentry families, eight freemen, and practically all the local tradesmen – the children of the baker, basket-maker, blacksmith, bootmaker, butcher, carpenter, coppersmith, currier, draper, fuller, glazier, inn-keeper, shoemaker, tailor, tanner, victualler, and even an undertaker. From outside the parish five more tradesmen sent their sons: a fellmonger, a chandler, a weaver, a grocer, and a Northampton shoemaker. During Cobb's time there were also the sons of three peers, twelve baronets or knights, four esquires, sixteen parsons, ten London merchants, thirty-two gentlemen, twenty freemen and nine farmers. Obviously the place was very democratic in character. The only hint of snobbishness that creeps in was the care with which Dugard distinguished social gradations, writing the names of the nobility in red ink. (At Eton they did the same.)

Rifling through the register, one finds among the earliest names that of Edward Maria Wingfield, nephew and namesake of the first president of the Colony of Virginia. Further on are the three Montague brothers. They were cousins of the Earl of Sandwich, and are frequently mentioned by Samuel Pepys in his *Diary* – the eldest was appointed as one of the commissioners to receive King Charles from the Scots; another became Attorney-General and Lord Chief Baron (his wife put Pepys 'in an ill humour all day' being apparently less beautiful than he had been led to expect). John Creed, whose name frequently occurs in Pepys' *Diary*, had a son at Oundle. Thomas Alleyn, the son of a Grocer, entered the school in 1630; afterwards, as Lord Mayor of London, he headed the procession which welcomed Charles II on his restoration. Oliver Luke, inscribed in 1634, was the son of the Sir Samuel Luke who is immortalised as the original of *Hudibras* by Samuel Butler (1612 – 1680), 'who knew what's what, and smelt a rat and looked a gift horse in the mouth'.

Many Oundelians took part in the Civil War: the three brothers of John Claypole, 'that debauched, ungodly Cavalier' who married Cromwell's favourite daughter Elizabeth, were not unnaturally on the Parliament side. There were also Royalists, such as Richard Washington, whose emigré cousin was the great-grandfather of George Washington.

Among other names which catch the eye is that of John Newton, who came to Oundle at the age of eight and was in the top form when Cobb died in 1537. Newton became Chaplain to Charles II. He wrote books to faciliate the use of logarithms, and was a strong advocate for educational reform, protesting against the tuition of nothing but Latin and Greek. There was scarcely a grammar school master competent to teach arithmetic or astronomy, he complained, adding that 'it is the want of mathematic learning that makes us so weak at Sea, and so deficient in the manual trades'.

These sentiments have a Sandersonian ring, and since Newton spent ten years at Oundle one wonders whether he was drawing on personal experience or thinking of the general state of grammar schools when he wrote scathingly:

I wish that the people of this Nation would consider how great a cheat too many of our Grammar Masters put upon them, to say nothing of our Writing-Masters, who yet are most of them as ignorant in Arithmetic, as our Grammar-Masters are of other sciences. But how, will some say, do Grammar-Masters put a cheat upon the people? Why thus, they cheat the parents of their money, and the children of their time, taking in the children to be instructed in the rudiments of the Latin tongue, before they can either write or read, and teaching them in a method quite contrary to what is prescribed in the Epistle usually printed before the common Accidence . . . But all they care for is the parents money, and as for the children, let them learn or be whipped: and thus they make more blockheads than ever God made, and ruin more children with their severe glister-pipes, than ever they made with their instructions.

There is no evidence that Cobb was either inefficient or brutal (though efficacious headmasters tended to be fervent floggers). But Newton's words serve as a reminder that school life at Oundle in the seventeenth century was still no Pestalozzian dream.

The hours were long, four hours in the morning and often five in the afternoon, with no more than one half-holiday a week. Very boring and incomprehensible the curriculum must have seemed to children destined to become artisans or farmers, and who would have agreed with Will Summers: 'Speech is the devil's *paternoster*. Nouns and pronouns, I pronounce you as traitors to boys' buttocks, *syntax* and *prosodia*, you are tormentors of wit and good for nothing but to get a schoolmaster twopence a week'. There were no terms, moreover, or even quarters, and holidays, all told, did not amount to more than twenty days a year.

Boys entered the school when their parents chose to send them, usually avoiding the winter months. Those who came as boarders, that is the great majority, lodged with the master or the usher, or with various families around the town. There was no organised sport, and the lads were left to their own devices in such spare time as they had. They played with hoops or tops, and roamed around the countryside, probably poaching.

It was a tough routine. To get through the school curriculum required years of hard study and long hours at hard benches subject to rigorous discipline. Understandably, many pupils gave up, preferring an easier life at home. Yet a large proportion went on to university, and as the tendency of the school, like that of the surrounding district, was towards Puritanism, many entered the Puritan Cambridge colleges of Emmanuel and Sidney Sussex.

When Cobb died in harness in 1637, the governors elected an old boy of the school to succeed him (in preference, as we noted, to Thomas Chaloner, who shortly afterwards became headmaster of Shrewsbury. But since Chaloner was deposed by Cromwell, his politics and religion may not have been in keeping with those of Oundle).

The successful candidate, Thomas Johnson, was the son of the vicar of Lilford; he was shown as being in the top form of the school when the Register opened. He gained his M.A. at Emmanuel College, Cambridge, in 1635, and six months after taking up his new appointment he married a local girl, Martha Nethercote.

Johnson arrived to find a junior schoolfellow of his, Strickland Negus, acting as usher, and seventy pupils, to which he added forty-seven others in his first year. In 1640 Negus left to get his M.A. at Cambridge, and another old boy, William Taylor, came as usher. Since Taylor's father had held that job under Spencer, it seems as though the Oundelian tradition was already strong. In 1638 and 1642 there were visitations, at both of which the governors were greeted by schoolboy orations and the examiners pronounced themselves satisfied.

Everything appeared to be going splendidly until the Civil War intervened. The battle of Naseby was fought in Northamptonshire on 14 June 1645, and the minutes of the Grocers' Company dated 18 June record that the visitation for that year would have to be cancelled due to 'the troubles of this kingdom and the danger of travelling'. At Oundle these troubles were reflected in a sudden reduction in numbers, as parents withdrew their children from what appeared to be a dangerous area of the country. Johnson himself may have been alarmed by developments, for he wrote to the Grocers in London saying that he had accepted a living and intended to leave Oundle; adding, somewhat sourly, that he had advised William Taylor not to apply for his post, as he regarded him unfit for the job.

Taylor did apply. But acting on the recommendation of the redoubtable Dr Busby of Westminster school, the governors appointed a young Westminster scholar who had just got his M.A. at Trinity College, Cambridge. The register shows that when William Hicks took over there were only 30 boys in the school. However, with the help of Samuel Jordan – appointed as usher by Hicks in his first week, and who remained for nineteen years – the numbers rapidly returned to normal. Between his arrival in September 1646 and August 1650, Hicks admitted ninety-five boys, and sent eight of his pupils to Cambridge.

Not bad, considering the prevailing unrest in the country. In March 1650 a party from Grocers' Hall, headed by Colonel Matthew Sheppard, made a visitation to Oundle. Once again it was a success and the visitors returned home with a high opinion of Hicks and Jordan. But then an awkward thing happened. It appeared that the vicar, Robert Resbury – a Calvinist who called himself not vicar but 'Minister of the Gospel in Oundle' – nursed a grudge. He was put out that Hicks had been chosen in preference to an acquaintance of his from Huntingdon. Hicks, though not in orders, was a Church of England man, and tension had grown up between them. Such animosity would normally have been unimportant. But Resbury was a friend of Cromwell, in whose eyes Oundle itself was 'this disaffected corner of the country'. Consequently the matter had to be taken seriously. And so, on Colonel Sheppard's insistance (his military rank must have played a part) the unfortunate Hicks was forced to resign.

The new Master was an Oxford graduate named William Griffiths, who left Leicester Grammar School because his salary was not being paid. During his seven years at Oundle

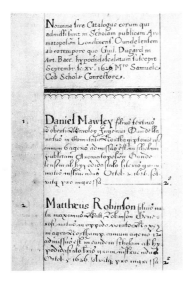

VERA EFFIGIES IOHANIS
NEWTON ÆTAT·39
1 6 6 0

The engraving of John Newton (left) is the oldest of an OO. (Far left) The first page of the School Register, begun in 1626.

harmony seems to have been re-established, for he admitted 87 boys (and Resbury's son was awarded an exhibition to Cambridge). But in 1657 Griffiths, in his turn, gave up the job to become rector of Polebrook, which suggests that a peaceful retreat in the countryside was preferable to teaching in the uneasy period of the Commonwealth.

At last William Taylor had his chance and, armed with a sheaf of testimonials from local worthies, he was duly elected. But though he had finally got what he wanted and was Master of his old school, the sixteen troubled years of his reign raised some suspicion that Johnson may have judged him correctly after all.

True, the deterioration of the school was not altogether his fault. Taylor could hardly be blamed for the slow decline of Puritanism after the Restoration of Charles II, or for the financial havoc caused by the Fire of London in 1666. Nor was he responsible for the waning interest in a classical education once promotion no longer depended solely on Latin. A man like John Newton would have known what to do, and busied himself with remedies; but sadly Taylor was not a person of that calibre.

Soon after his appointment came the death of Oliver Cromwell. The Montagues played their part in the Restoration, and, as we said, the Lord Mayor who welcomed Charles II back was a Grocer who had been educated at Oundle. The return of the monarchy meant changes at Grocers' Hall (Colonel Sheppard was elbowed out) and had repercussions at Oundle, which became a refuge for nonconformists. Resbury resigned from his ministry and took to practising medicine, apparently with such success that people flocked to his house – though chiefly, perhaps, because it was licenced for preaching. And William Hicks appealed to be reinstated as Master.

Though the Governors kept Taylor on, he must have had an anxious time. Above all,

(Above) Grocers' Hall as it was restored after the Fire of London

there was a constant worry about funds for the school. The Grocers had been economising ever since they had been forced to make loans to Charles I to pay off the Scots in 1640, and three years later for the defence of London. This 'Ship Money' had to be borrowed, and very little of their loans had been repaid by the time of the Restoration, which itself led to further demands on the City. Yet if the Company was financially embarrassed, there was no reason to fear disaster. So far as Oundle was concerned, it meant that by 1666 payments were just a quarter behind.

Then came the Fire of London. Thirteen thousand houses were destroyed, including all those on the lands bequeathed by Laxton. Grocers' Hall was burnt out; only the garden tower containing the records escaped the flames. Practically everything the Company owned was gutted, except for a few small houses in Grub Street; even Laxton's tomb disappeared. It was a disastrous blow: the Grocers owed over twenty thousand pounds – many millions in modern terms – and there was little prospect of encashing their own credits.

Faced with this appalling situation the Company gave proof of its resilience. During the first difficult years after the fire, payments to Oundle were delayed rather than suspended.

This meant, in effect, that the school received only half its normal income, even if the arrears were later made up. In the meantime numbers fell and the intake of new pupils shrank. All this imposed a severe strain on Taylor who, if not actually starving, was forced to pull in his belt uncomfortably tight. The usher left, and when rumours reached London that Taylor was about to defect, the Master of the Grocers' Company himself hurried to see what was going wrong with the school.

He was greeted by lamentations in Latin from the boys, and a disheartened Master. In the opinion of the town, Taylor was worn out and no longer capable of conducting the school properly. When the wardens found that he had a church living in view and was only staying on until he had received his arrears, they promised to settle the account and gave him a year to leave.

This leisurely notice was necessary because they had no one to take his place. Later in the year, however, two applications were received. Their choice fell on William Speed of Gibson's school, Ratcliffe, an institution with which the Grocers were connected.

If Speed was the only headmaster of Oundle who failed to satisfy Laxton's requirement of being an M.A., he was also the only one to have published a volume of Latin verse. (Though intending to go into orders, he had apparently matriculated at Christ Church, Oxford, but left without taking a degree.) Sad to say, he too lived through seventeen years of financial anxiety and departed, partially unpaid, in 1689.

The reason for this sorry state of affairs was that the Grocers' Company administered a number of charities, and when payments fell into arrears some of them reacted by biting the hand that was struggling to feed them. The governors of Christ's Hospital went so far as to seize Grocers' Hall. Subsequently the sequestrated building was mortgaged for two hundred pounds a year by Sir John Moore to be used as the Lord Mayor's residence. It would be tedious to go into all the tortuous details of how the Grocers eventually overcame their difficulties; suffice it to say that they became solvent again and liquidated all their debts. Actually, Speed deserted the ship just as the tide rose to lift her off the rocks, though he could hardly have realised this at the time. Meanwhile everyone had to make shift as best he could.

There were about forty boys at Oundle when Speed took over, and in his first year he admitted thirty-three others, so there was no reason to complain about numbers. Unhappily some of them were not very bright. Maybe Taylor had been obliged to scrape a few barrels to keep the place going, and admitted pupils who were too weak to cope with a classical education. When sifting out the dross, Speed made epigrammatic little notes in the Register ('long he overstayed his leave, at last he left to stay at home') which afford some tantalising little cameos. One boy of eleven left to go to a writing school ('a blockhead who will never make a scholar'); another aged seventeen went to an attorney's office. A lad of twelve went to a merchant's, another to a bakery at Thrapston, a third to work in a chemist's shop. After nine years at the school one Henry Boteler went up to Magdalene College, Cambridge at the age of seventeen, and a sixteen-year-old joined the Inns of Court. The two sons of Sir Oliver St John, Bart., aged fourteen and sixteen, were expelled for being 'incorrigible rebels'. Another nuisance of fifteen was dispatched *post correctionem* – presumably a flogging (which the incorrigible brothers seem to have escaped). A few years later a Nottinghamshire parson's son was expelled for getting a girl pregnant, and there are hints that the system of boarding boys out in the town led to more than just truancy and disobedience. Occasionally there is a personal vignette, for instance of a boy leaving at eighteen and a half: 'at last full of years and exceedingly tall he said goodbye to school and now pursues country matters in Lincolnshire'. Speed discontinued these leaving notes after the first few years. Nevertheless a pattern emerges. Older boys of fifteen or sixteen go to London to be apprenticed; some move on to the universities or to other schools; the younger ones leave to help their fathers in their trades. Such were the seventeenth-century Old Oundelians.

By contrast the Grocers' records are filled with Speed's petitions for money and arguments over whether he was right to claim the usher's salary (which was included in his own sixty pound stipend) during the long periods when he made do without an assistant. Every so often he appeared in person to press for payment, but nevertheless his salary was often in arrears. When only ten pounds was paid to him in 1689, he finally lost patience and decamped to open a private school of his own in Hampstead. How this venture fared is unknown; but the records at Grocers' Hall show that in the end he received all that was due to him.

Actually the Grocers first learnt of Speed's departure from Mr Strickson, the Oundle hatter, on one of his visits to London. At his suggestion they asked the new vicar, Edward Caldwell, to take charge until a successor to Speed could be found. Mr Strickson thought that Caldwell was just the man to restore the school's credit. And as things turned out, there was little other choice; no candidate appeared as a suitable alternative. Thus shortly after being instituted as vicar at Oundle (in addition to being rector of nearby Pilton) the Rev. Edward Caldwell also became Master of Oundle School, partly in deference to local opinion, but also in the hope that his appointment would lead to the school's recovery.

The trend towards appointing clergymen as schoolmasters at grammar schools was very much a feature of the eighteenth century, and usually resulted in their atrophy if not extinction. Since this is precisely what happened (or very nearly happened) to Oundle, it is perhaps appropriate to endorse Walker's dictum that in so far as the school was concerned, the new century began in 1689.

V
'WHAT'S YOUR NAME AND WHO'S YOUR FATHER?'
THE EIGHTEENTH CENTURY

'WHOSOEVER will examine the state of the grammar schools in different parts of the kingdom', observed Lord Kenyon dispassionately in 1795, 'will see to what a lamentable condition most of them are reduced. If all persons had equally done their duty, we should not find, as is now the case, empty walls without scholars, and everything neglected but the receipt of salaries and emoluments.'

At the time he voiced this criticism many of the old endowed schools had come under the control of clergymen – decorous divines who already had parishes or benefices to look after, and were torpidly content to neglect their scholastic responsibilities. Some were just idle, or incompetent; others ruined the school by deliberately restricting the number of pupils and pocketing the endowment. Often the vicar or rector complacently added the headmaster's pay to his income and left the teaching to a cut-rate curate. In the absence of examinations or indeed inspections, such men lingered on well beyond normal retirement age. The eighteenth century was a period of long headmasterships in comfortable but decaying sinecures. Oundle was not the only educational establishment where sleeping dons were allowed to die.

Inherently the problem was that endowed schools, being bound by ancient statutes to a classical curriculum, taught nothing but Latin and Greek. It was still illegal for them to teach other subjects. True, this régime produced a handful of dazzling scholars. But for the majority of children it meant a routine of sheer drudgery, of little practical use to boys who were destined to become merchants or farmers and play a part in the Industrial Revolution that was already gaining strength.

Consequently many parents gave up sending their sons to grammar schools. Some of them preferred to employ private tutors; others made use of the hundreds of private commercial schools that were springing up all over the country. ('It was not uncommon' observed the itinerant Swiss, Pastor Moritz, 'to see a succession of signs on doors saying "children educated here" just like "shoes mended here".') Protestant boys from nonconformist families went to Dissenting Academies which, being bound by no charters, were able to offer a more varied curriculum, blending classical studies with subjects such as geography and mathematics, history and modern languages. Students were taught natural science, and even shorthand; there was emphasis on speaking correct English, on spelling and handwriting. Moreover for the first time we hear of girls' schools, such as the one set up at Newington Green by Mary Wollstonecraft. Since polite society didn't take female minds too seriously, these schools groomed girls for their role in the world, teaching the arts and graces along with reading and sewing and perhaps a little French. (Jane Austen attended three of them, though she picked up most of her education from her clergyman father.)

If some liberal families chose these new establishments in preference to the diet of 'birch, boorishness, buggery and the bottle' which characterised the great public schools, it was nevertheless clear that the classics opened doors for preferment and were part of a gentleman's education. Classical knowledge was absolutely necessary, Lord Chesterfield told his son, because everyone agreed to think so. The advantages were twofold, remarked Thomas Gaisford: 'It enables us to look down with contempt on those who have not shared its advantages, and also fits us for places of emolument, not only in this world, but in that which is to come.'

But the public schools, which were of course not public at all, since very little of what went on in them was intentionally revealed, had acquired an unenviable reputation. The main charge brought against them, and directed by no less a person than the Master of the Temple (himself an Etonian) was that of sin – with a capital S. Adding his voice, Sydney Smith, who had been Captain of the School at Westminster, wrote in the influential *Edinburgh Review* that in his opinion they offered 'premature debauchery that only prevents men from being corrupted by the world by corrupting them before they entered the world'. The public schools, he said, were a system of abuse, neglect and vice in which a boy began as a slave and was likely to end up himself as a tyrant. Henry Fielding, who had been at Eton, made one of his disgruntled characters call them 'the nurseries of all vice and immorality'.

Every aspect of the public schools was denounced – fagging, boy government, corporal punishment, unsupervised social liberty, immutability of the dead languages and so forth – the very elements, in fact, which they themselves venerated as part of the traditional process of a gentleman's education. The protagonists regarded themselves as part of an élite society, which by its nature kept the outside world at a distance. They were a separate caste, whose mystic had evolved from the feudal past and mirrored the attitudes and values of a robust, land-owning gentry. This governing class had its own terms of admission and adherence, and schools such as Westminster, Winchester or Eton were designed to forge a bond of shared manners and outlook that united its members in a gentlemanly caste.

In plainer language Thomas Hughes has Tom Brown's father say, as he dispatches his son to Rugby: 'Shall I tell him he's sent to school to make himself a good scholar? . . . Well but he isn't . . . I don't care a straw for Greek particles or for the digamma, no more than does his mother . . . If he'll only turn out to be a brave, helpful, truth-telling Englishman, and a gentleman and a Christian, that's all I want.'

But it was certainly an uncomfortable process, a trial by ordeal. Every newcomer had to go through the mill: there was no respect for rank. The fifth Marquess of Londonderry used to tell the story that when he first appeared at Eton dressed in white trousers and a light blue jacket with frills, an older boy came up and asked: 'What's your name, and who's your father?' He replied: 'I am Charles Stuart Vane, Viscount Seaham, and my father is the Marquess of Londonderry'. Whereupon the other gave him three tremendous kicks – one for Vane, one for Seaham, and one for Londonderry.

For a small boy arriving at the bottom of the public school hierarchy, life was undeniably tough. At Rugby the initiation ceremonies involved running the gauntlet between rows of executioners armed with knotted hankerchiefs, and being stoned with rolls baked as hard as pebbles. New boys had to stand on a table and sing; the penalty for failing to give a satisfactory performance was to swallow a pail of muddy water crammed full of salt, which often made the victims ill for days. At Harrow the new boys were tossed in a blanket (a certain number of bumps on the ceiling being necessary to validate the ceremony) and this was followed by the ritual of pinching, an art which had been developed into such a painful form of torture that one wretched child sought refuge up the chimney and had to be dragged out choking with soot and almost insane with terror. At Winchester the cruelties were formalised. The tradition of 'tin gloves' required the lad's hand to be hardened by searing it with a burning brand of wood. In later life a clergyman re-called 'the grinding thrill of pain as the glowing wood was pressed on it by the ministering fiend'.

Since the boys were left to their own devices outside the classroom, bullying was inevitable and often sickening. Southey wrote that a friend of his was taken away from Charterhouse because he was almost killed there by the bigger boys. 'They used to lay him before the fire till he was scorched, and shut him in a trunk with sawdust till he had nearly expired from suffocation. The Charterhouse at that time was a sort of hell on earth for the younger boys.'

Bullying led to fagging and the prefect system. The senior boys forced the juniors to become their slaves, and leathered into them if they resisted. There were so few masters that they could do whatever they liked. To counter the problem, the authorities roped in the seniors to maintain discipline. These monitors or prefects, call them what you will, became unpaid ushers, with fags as unpaid servants. It was a convenient way of securing free labour. By the eighteenth century the system had become institutionalised and fagging was a hallowed tradition.

How wretched a small boy's life was in Georgian days can only be conjectured, for such matters tended to be veiled in secrecy. We know that Shelley, whose earliest extant writing is his name carved boldly on his desk, loathed Eton and rebelled continually against fagging. Yet it was not as harsh at Eton as at some other schools. An anonymous writer, quoted by John Chandos, painted a lurid picture of the little Wykehamist fags, forced to fight for a place in front of the fire to toast their masters' bread, being 'lashed by a large brute with a whip', and Samuel Rogers recounts that Lord Holland was forced by his fagmaster to make toast with his bare hands, as a result of which his fingers became permanently misshapen.

It was a vicious world, this little universe of self-governing boys. As late as 1842

Thackeray observed that 'there are at this present time of writing five hundred boys at Eton, kicked and licked, and bullied by another hundred – scrubbing shoes, running errands, making false concords and (as if that were a natural consequence) putting their posteriors on a block for Dr Hawtrey to lash at; and still calling it education.' A contributor to the *Westminster Journal* thought that 'to black shoes under the penalty of being beaten for non-compliance, is slavery in man or boy.' Indeed at Shrewsbury the fags were known as 'dowls', a word supposedly derived from the ancient Greek for 'slave'.

In Arabic it would have been *mam'luk*, and the public school conventions bear a striking resemblance to those of the Mamelukes in medieval Egypt. In *Napoleon to Nasser* I noted:

> Once sold by his family – or as likely as not simply kidnapped from his village in the Caucasus by a dealer – the young boy would find himself with a shipload of others like himself heading for Cairo where, naked in the slave market, he would wait to be bought by one of the Mameluke Beys. The break with his family and his home was complete; he had now lost his identity and even his religion and become a member of a military caste with strict rules and conventions. Yet although living in the cellars of the Bey's palace, he would find himself regarded as a sort of adopted child in his master's household regiment, loyal to his Bey and his fellow-slaves, and trained, as part of an élite fraternity, to despise *fellahin* and civilians alike, and even to look down on marriage and family life as fatal to his profession of a man at arms.
>
> If luck was on his side, the young mameluke would be sent to a military school where he would be taught to read and write, learn the Koran, and be drilled in the arts of warfare. Contact with the outside world was forbidden, and discipline was strict – enforced by a sort of prefectorial system, the older recruits, known as *Aghas* (big brothers) being in charge of the rest. While at school, the mameluke received no pay and had no rights; but once he had graduated he would be ceremoniously granted his freedom.

Every Sultan and every Bey went through the ranks on their way to the Citadel, and were proud of it too (some even adopted their former *Agha's* name.)

Most English boys probably shared the same romantic if masochistic sensations, though they had precious little to be thankful for in the old unreformed public schools. Accommodation was appalling; the old barn-like dormitory at Westminster was said to be 'not much better for juniors than casuals at a "union" workhouse.' Edward Thring has described the horrors of the notorious Long Chamber at Eton. 'After eight o'clock at night,' he wrote, 'no prying eye came near until the following morning, no one lived in the same building; cries of joy and pain were equally unheard; excepting a code of laws of their own, there was no help or redress for anyone.'

The cold, the dirt, the discomfort, and the lack of privacy were bad enough, but what chills the blood is the thought of those interminable nights of bullying and beastliness when boys aged from nine to nineteen were locked up together and left to their own resources. The food, too, was filthy, and there was never enough of it. The younger boys at the end of the queue suffered most, and would often have gone starving but for hampers from home.

Yet there would be a sequel to those dark days. In due course the child who had been knocked about and fagged in every direction would be elevated from slave to oligarch on the principle of 'Do unto others what was done to thyself', and able to frighten the juniors in his turn – a process which seemed to act as a magical elixir for previous hardships.

When they were not oppressing one another, inmates at the great boarding schools were free from adult authority to a degree that now seems extraordinary. 'Sat up all night with three other fellows swigging wine and playing cards,' boasts a fifteen year-old Wykehamist in his diary. 'Shirked chapel next morning, told looked unwell. At four o'clock a great bowl of punch with Shedderson. At night after tutor had gone round we grubbed a cold goose up in our room, having no plates we ate off the back of our basins which gave it a great flavour, aided by a comfortable bowl of punch.'

Appetites were sharpened by forays on neighbouring chambers. At the age of thirteen, Thomas Arnold wrote to his aunt that his quarters were 'very subject to sieges'.

> Lipscomb coming into the chamber and beginning the Assault & the Forces of the Enemy increasing, I sprung out of Bed, and girding a Blanket about me, & standing up on my Bed gave & sustained a most dreadful Fire – Loaves of Crum of Bread, Washing Boxes, Candles, Candle Sticks, the Broom & every kind of missile Weapon was hurl'd without Distinction; I received a wound on my head from a washing box, but my Pericranium being far harder than any stone, the Washing Box rebounded; the only damage I sustained was in my Bed, which was not only pulled to pieces entirely, but so covered with Crumbs, Candles &c, that I was oblig'd to make it again completely.

A few years later this frisky lad became the headmaster of Rugby who felt that he was surrounded by 'a mass of evil' a thousand times worse than 'all the idolatry of India'. Arnold's Winchester saw four rebellions between 1770 and 1793, and in 1818, a decade after he left, the prefects staged a revolt against Dr Gabell. Boys barricaded themselves into a part of the school and withstood the police for twenty-four hours. Only after the militia were called in and advanced with fixed bayonets did the mutineers surrender.

Uprisings of this sort were usually a trial of strength, and took place when the school authorities attempted to curtail the prefects' privileges. In this case a prefect had flogged a boy senseless. The school doctor told the headmaster he was lucky not to have a corpse on his hands, and the prefect, a certain Goodenough, was expelled. Significantly, Goodenough was not in the least penitent for what he had done; on the contrary, he was indignant at being taken to task, and the rest of the school backed him up. They were apparently not prepared to submit to adult rule outside the classroom.

At Winchester the Praefect of Hall's powers were almost unlimited. (It was said that there were three absolute rulers in the world – the Great Mogul, the captain of a man-of-war, and the Praefect of Hall at Winchester.) He could flog any boy on the spot, and frequently did so with relish. Even as late as 1872 there was still no limit to the number of strokes a prefect might inflict at 'tunding'.

In the Middle Ages it was unknown for boys to inflict corporal punishment on one another; this was left to the Master. And goodness knows, the great heads were nearly all ferocious floggers. Udall, headmaster of Eton in the sixteenth century, was notorious for the savagery of his beatings. Cook, the High Master of St Paul's, laid into one boy so hard that he kept the scars for the rest of his life. Moss of Shrewsbury once gave his victim 88 lashes. Keate and Arnold, Vaughan and Butler, continued to indulge in the same institutionalised cruelty. So did practically every other headmaster, sometimes with unfortunate side affects. Foreigners called this passion for flagellation *le vice anglais*, and Henry Spencer Ashbee affirmed in 1879 that 'the secret propensity which the English most cherish is undoubtedly flagellation'. For this curious perversion the old public schools must, regrettably, bear much of the blame; nor does it come as a surprise to learn that some of the most celebrated offenders – Udall, Vaughan et al – were forced to resign for indulging in sexual misdemeanours with boys in their charge.

So why did parents put up with such barbaric treatment of their children? Partly it was because of ignorance; the system of brutality in boarding schools was protected by a taboo of silence which boys feared to break. Partly it was because they joined the boys in laughing it all off as part of the cheerful anarchy of school life, as this piece of Etoniana shows:

I had continually Horses lent me by a Friend at Windsor . . . On one occasion met with another Boy Lord Berkeley's Hounds from Cranford Bridge at Sydenham Copse – chopped a Vixen – the Dog took us over Chalvey ditch to Salt Hill – Black Park – almost to Beaconsfield – back to Burnham Beeches – ran short there – Bulstrode Park – long check there – the Fox seen by a Farmer between two fat hog's shoulders – a very good run – got a pad – knew I should be flogged – two Praeposters waiting to seize me at my Dames – galloped thro' Eton – the Masters at dinner – was seized and Dr Davies waiting at home to flog me; had my desert before dinner – five or six to meet us at the Christopher – Mr Kendal's superexcellent Port to drink success to Foxhunting . . .

But one of the main reasons for the brutality was simply greed. Headmasters kept their teaching staff small to have more money available for themselves and the charmed circle around them. (During the eighteenth century Eton was practically a private fief of two or three families.) The disproportion between masters and boys was astonishing – three or four masters taught several hundred boys in one huge hall. To maintain even a semblance of order among so many lads, some of them rich and rumbustious, was no easy job; and outside the classroom they were virtually uncontrolled. Consequently the only way to govern the ungovernable was by unremitting terror. And terror was sustained by the rod.

Understandably, the more boisterous elements often got out of hand. Drunkenness was commonplace and there was little pretence that the older boys did not consort with whores

– in fact girls came from as far away as Coventry to solicit at Rugby School. When an assistant master at Shrewsbury complained that immorality with women was very common among the seniors, Butler replied that the only thing to do was try and keep it in check. Even the much admired Dr Barnard had little illusions about his charges at Eton. Belabouring Lord Hinchingbrooke for getting a girl pregnant, he exclaimed after a few lashes: 'Psha! What signifies my flogging him for being like his father? What's bred in the bone will never get out of the flesh.'

Indeed the whole attitude towards sex was casual and permissive. The Sixth form ran a brothel at Eton, and though homosexuality undoubtedly existed – attractive youngsters were known as 'bitches' at Harrow and 'tarts' at Winchester – the subject rarely attracted much attention, perhaps because it was too commonplace to excite comment, or possibly because incest was the *frisson* of the age. There was far more talk of prize-fighting.

Though the 'noble art' was unlawful, it was highly esteemed and even condoned in schools. Well into the nineteenth century boys fought each other bloodily on any pretext, and hardly a day passed, according to Gladstone, 'without one, two, three, or even four more or less mortal combats'.

Sometimes they were indeed lethal. In December 1784 the *London Chronicle* carried an account of a fight between two Eton boys in which one was killed and the other seriously hurt. The most famous encounter took place in 1825 when Lord Shaftesbury's youngest son, Francis Ashley, lost his life after a fight lasting two hours. No one was punished and public opinion applauded Lord Shaftesbury for not arraigning his son's opponent for manslaughter. Since there were no organised games at any public school until well into the nineteenth century, the Duke of Wellington's old tag about the battle of Waterloo being won on the playing fields of Eton ('*C'est ici qu'a été gagnée la bataille de Waterloo*') can only have meant the arena in which the boys fought each other.

If for all their shortcomings the public schools managed to thrive, it was chiefly due to the efforts of certain headmasters. Rugby, for instance, owed its rise in the social scale not merely to the increase in value of its endowments, but principally to the appointment of Dr James from Eton. By 1780 Rugby had become recognised as one of the great schools. Shrewsbury was rescued by a Rugby master when it was on its last legs – there were only 18 boys when Samuel Butler arrived. Christ's Hospital and Charterhouse were also resuscitated by able eighteenth-century headmasters.

At the same time a good many of the old grammar schools declined through lack of a good man at the helm. Manchester Grammar School's numbers dropped from 548 to 288 during a period when the city's population more than doubled. Berkhamstead, which had started with 144 boys in 1523, went down to ten. In 1750 Bromsgrove was one of the largest schools in the Midlands. By 1818 only 12 pupils remained, and the clergyman in charge of them was usually to be seen drunk in the local pub. Repton, which had 300 scholars at the end of the seventeenth century, was reduced to 'only a few ragged boys'.

Sedbergh, once a thriving north country establishment, was unlucky enough to have a series of hopeless pedagogues. The first became a recluse and refused to see anybody. The next was such a ninny that the boys pulled his nose. A later one threw out all the boarders because he disliked having them in his house. When a Charity commissioner paid a visit in the 1860s, he found the place reduced to a delapidated village school with only four or five boys. 'As to Sedbergh,' he wrote in his report, 'I despair of putting it into any class at all. In its present state it simply cumbers the ground.'

Sadly, a similar deterioration took place at Oundle. As we have seen, Oundle had grown from an ancient endowed foundation to become one of the leading grammar schools in the country during the reign of Charles I. Though not as fashionable as Westminster or Winchester or Eton, it was certainly in the same league as Rugby or Shrewsbury. As Mack wrote:

> From the first it was partially a boarding school, and in the course of its long history, had several periods when it was to all intents and purposes a public school, though – significantly enough – it always emphasised science more than did the average public school. In 1626 the School claimed 100 boarders, ranging from undertakers to baronets, and sent many boys to Cambridge. After the Restoration, fire, plague and a political atmosphere uncongenial to a school with Puritan sympathies caused decline and finally extinction. When Oundle was revived in 1796, it taught chiefly the technical sciences and practical subjects, but from 1830 to 1876 it settled down as an ordinary successful country Grammar school.
>
> (E.C.Mack, Public Schools and British Opinion since 1860)

From 1689 until 1796 Oundle was affected by the same blight that characterised so many other old endowed schools, which Sir Joshua Fitch described as 'inefficient supervision on the part of the Governing Bodies, and languor and feebleness on the part of teachers and taught'.

The Grocers' Company, preoccupied with their financial problems, were content to leave the school in the hands of the local vicar. But the Rev. Edward Caldwell seems to have regarded the job simply as an additional benefice. He appointed Edward Battie, a fellow of King's, as usher, and when Battie returned to his old school, Eton, as a conduct two years later, the job of usher was passed on to Caldwell's son. In his first year he received nine boys, and during the following years an average of eight. Of the total intake during Caldwell's period of office, thirty were town boys, thirty-two came from the adjoining countryside (including the sons of six local parsons) and sixteen arrived from London, Dublin, Cheshire, and Canterbury. Five are recorded as having gone on to Cambridge before Caldwell stopped keeping up the Register. (He also failed to maintain his parish register at Pilton.)

Complaints about his slackness reached Grocers' Hall, but nothing was done until Caldwell's death in 1718. At that point the disillusioned governors decided to appoint a professional schoolmaster rather than see who took his place as vicar of Oundle. They chose

View of the Town Church and Bridge of Oundle taken in Ascheton Field to the North

(Above) *The 'View of the Town Church and Bridge of Oundle taken in Ascheton Field to the North' dates from 1721. This sepia-wash drawing is now in the British Museum.*

a fellow of St John's named John Jones, who was in orders and reading for his B.C.L. (Bachelor of Civil Law). Jones was a bright young scholar who might very well have pulled the school together. But he was eager for ecclesiastic preferment and left soon after getting his degree. All we know about his time at Oundle is that he found both the schoolhouse and the master's house in a dilapidated condition. Caldwell, having a rectory at Pilton and a vicarage at Oundle, had not bothered about repairs.

John Jones made no entries in the register, and since his successor had the same surname it is difficult to identify which boys were with whom. The new master, Richard Jones, came from Kettering Grammar School and was also rector of Glendon. Since he was the only applicant, the governors were once again obliged to appoint a clergyman, and a middle-aged one at that, who already had a living. Ominously enough, he thereupon became vicar of Weekley as well.

Once again the school was treated as a sinecure. For a good deal of Richard Jones' long tenure there is evidence of boys and indeed potential scholars, but no traces of an usher. The school simply vegetated. Despite occasional petitions from the local inhabitants, the schoolmaster's house was allowed to fall into ruin. When Richard Jones died, it had to be completely rebuilt. Admittedly a man of eighty-seven does not usually make an active headmaster, whatever he once was, and it is hardly surprising that the next man to hold the job, Samuel Murthwaite, headed his section of the Register: 'The Public School of Oundle for long badly attended'.

One wonders whether he found any pupils at all, for the governors took ten months to make the appointment, during which time there was not even a caretaker at the school. At first the new Master (St Bees and St John's College, Cambridge) showed some acumen. He arranged for the schoolmaster's house to be rebuilt. Down came the Wyatt's old building and by 1763 the house on the corner of Church Lane was ready for Murthwaite and any boarders he could find. But only ten names were recorded in the register – two Londoners and eight boys from Oundle. For years he had but a handful of pupils, and only William Walcott, the son of the Oundle doctor, continued his studies after leaving the school. Murthwaite, one suspects, was not a man with much éclat. He also served as curate to the local vicar, and when the opportunity arose for him to become vicar of Desborough he left Oundle in 1778 as moribund as he had found it.

The man who replaced him was a more awkward customer. John Evanson came from a schoolmastering family and took his MA at Brasenose College, Oxford, in 1775. He was twenty-six and unmarried when he received four pupils from Murthwaite and made his own first entry in the Register. This was John Smith, the eldest son of a farmer and brewer from Stoke, who four years previously had founded the well-known Oundle brewery.

Either through laziness, or because there were none to inscribe, Evanson did not bother to enter any other names. After a while, however, complaints reached the governors that Evanson had found a tenant, and was proposing to rent the new schoolmaster's house. Interviewed in London, he was threatened with dismissal. But the incident served to remind the governors of their own responsibilities. Though the statutes required a visitation to be made every three years, the Company's records showed that none had taken place for the last 117 years.

Hastening to rectify the omission, they found seven boarders and three day-boys at Oundle, and expressed their wish to see the school restored to its former prosperity. Money was promised, and smart new uniforms were ordered for the almsmen.

This burst of liberality prompted Evanson to ask for an increase in salary. He also applied for permission to turn the institution into an elementary school which, by teaching writing and arithmetic, would be of more use to the community than the existing curriculum. Both requests were turned down.

At best Evanson cannot have had more than a dozen pupils, and in his opinion the suggestions made sense. When they were refused, he became embittered. Stories began to circulate about his queer behaviour. It was said that he made faces at people, clenched his fist, beat on doors. He shambled around the town with his breeches unbuttoned. Was he queer in the head, or had he become a drunkard?

That he was brutal, everyone knew; he beat and kicked his pupils unmercifully. One boy had his ears pulled so hard that they had to be bandaged for a month. Another was flogged

Bullen's foundation stone (above) *for a new building (now the east wing of the Cloisters) symbolised the revival of the School's fortunes at the end of the eighteenth century.*

senseless. Such violence was normal in schools, as we have seen. But here the parents were on the spot. Half Oundle inspected the bruises, and the governors received so many complaints that another visitation was ordered.

This time their enquiry was exhaustive and ran to many thousands of words. It concluded that Evanson was not deranged in mind, but unfit to be a schoolmaster. No one in Oundle would send his children to him. Yet significantly the main point at issue was less his severity than the high charges he made for teaching writing and arithmetic.

So Evanson was summoned before the governors and sacked. He responded with the threat of legal action for wrongful dismissal, and in the end was bought off with a payment of £250 (which under the circumstances sounds generous). Yet if nine months went by between the decision to get rid of Evanson and his departure, there was an even longer interval before the election of his successor took place. The Court did belatedly think of 'paying some attention to the youthful inhabitants of Oundle' but still dragged its feet. For twenty months there was neither master nor boy at the school – the longest break in its history. The routine appointments of overseers were made, but the selection of a headmaster was deferred.

The reason for this delay, however, was that the governors were proposing to revive the school with a radical programme of education. Latin would continue to be taught, of course, but much greater emphasis would be given to English and mathematics, as well as geography. More important still, a course of technical science would be introduced. Scholars were to receive ' a competent idea of the several manufactures and the metals from the rude material and the mines to their last improvement'. This was far ahead of the times for a grammar school, to be sure, and the problem facing the Court was how to carry out the new curriculum within the terms of the original endowment.

By March 1796 the governors felt confident about their tactics and appointed the Rev. Thomas Bullen of Christ's College, Cambridge as headmaster. Bullen quickly proved himself the right man to execute the project. On his arrival in June he found the buildings repaired, but not a single pupil at the school. However, that soon changed. By Christmas there were twenty-three boys – five of them former pupils of Evanson's – and at the end of Bullen's first year the overseers sent in a glowing report on the new headmaster's activities. Numbers had reached forty-five, of which twenty-one were boarders. Boys had come from all parts of the country, and included one from Jamaica. The new curriculum was turning out to be a great success; in addition to Latin and Greek, English grammar, arithmetic, merchant's accounts, surveying, geography and drawing were being taught by Bullen and his able assistant, Thomas Dix (who published a book on surveying which was used in the school for many years). Nor were the cleanliness, health, and morals of the boys being neglected. There was even the suggestion of a waiting list: 'From the application lately made for admissions, Mr Bullen has reason to believe that the number of his boarders might be considerably increased, did the size of his house enable him to accommodate them'.

It was certainly a remarkable renaissance, and shows that two centuries ago – at roughly the same period as Samuel Butler was reviving Shrewsbury and Dr James was putting Rugby on the map – the special identity of Oundle, the Oundelian character if you like, was already in the making. This was the start: a century later, Sanderson would bring it to maturity.

VI
THE FORMATION OF CHARACTER

UNTIL THE MID-NINETEENTH CENTURY there were only seven public schools in the whole of England. In fact, some purists would say only five. What's more, the term 'public school' was still rarely heard. There were the great schools, the grammar schools, and the rest.

Eton, Winchester and Westminster formed a triad with a recognisable character of their own, an aristocratic flavour, one might say. Towards the end of the eighteenth century they were joined by Harrow and Rugby, both of which aspired to offer a classical education to children of the higher ranks of society. This nucleus of five was subsequently extended to include Charterhouse (founded in 1611 to educate the sons of poor gentlemen) and Shrewsbury, after it had been brilliantly revived by Samuel Butler.

These seven made up a sort of club, though Westminster refused to play Charterhouse at cricket until 1850, and in 1866 turned down a challenge from Shrewsbury on the specious grounds that it was not a recognised public school. (Another story goes that when Eton was challenged by Rugby, the Eton captain's response was 'Rugby, Rugby . . . well, we'll think about it if you tell me where it is'.) St Paul's and Merchant Taylors', though predominantly day-schools, were such ancient foundations that they were often bracketed with the seven.

Each of these institutions had a distinctive clientele. Eton still catered for the landed gentry, and only latterly recruited boys from families with professional or business backgrounds. Harrow followed a similar though slightly more metropolitan pattern; its lack of religious discrimination later led to a notable connection with powerful Jewish families and Indian potentates. Winchester was more intellectual; Rugby concentrated on the clergy and the Midlands gentry rather more than the great aristocracy. In short, with the exception of St Paul's, which relied on the lower and middle classes, this coterie of schools almost exclusively served the top ranks of society right up until the reign of Queen Victoria. However, once the Industrial Revolution had got under way and the 1832 Reform Bill was passed, the social scene shifted. The landowning, fox-hunting gentry who had hitherto thrived on income from their estates or properties and scorned the idea of working for a living, began to acquire business interests and reluctantly put their sons into the professions. In contrast – and this was perhaps the vital difference between aristocratic and bourgeois attitudes – the middle classes extolled the work ethos as a virtue and amassed huge fortunes by exercising their earning capacities.

But once he had made his pile, the ambitious merchant or manufacturer began to realise that idleness was a badge of status. If he wanted his family to rise socially it was necessary (and indeed agreeable) to adopt the style of the upper ranks. 'At the heart of the bourgeois dream was the ideal of gracious living, symbolised by the country house,' observes the sociologist Houghton; 'the middle-class businessman longed to escape from drudgery in hideous surroundings into a world of beauty and leisure, a life of dignity and peace, from which sordid anxieties were shut out.'

An essential ingredient in this upward mobility was a classical education. Going through the mill of a public school conferred an imprimatur that made up for the lack of armorial bearings, often establishing a child's place in society more clearly than his family background was likely to do. 'Make no mistake about it,' Sir James Darling, the distinguished Old Reptonian headmaster of Geelong Grammar told me recently, 'the middle classes sent their sons to smart boarding schools for purely snobbish reasons.'

Certainly the growth of the middle classes accounted for the sudden plethora of new public schools that sprang up at the start of the Victorian age. Cheltenham, Marlborough, Rossal, Radley, Lancing, Brighton and Hurstpierpoint were all founded in the years between 1840 and 1849. Clifton followed in 1852, Epsom in 1855. Haileybury was originated by the East India Company; Wellington was created as a monument for the Iron Duke, largely on the initiative of the Prince Consort. Altogether twenty-three Anglican and eight public schools of other denominations came into existence during the first three decades of Queen Victoria's reign. Moreover similar foundations sprang up all over the British Empire, from the Indian sub-continent to Australia and New Zealand. It may come as a surprise to learn that King's College, Sydney; Melbourne and Geelong Grammar; St Peter's Adelaide; as well as Christ's College, Christchurch; Wanganni Collegiate and King's College, Auckland, are coevals of many English public schools, and that the Singapore, or Raffles Institution, founded by Sir Stamford Raffles in 1823, is even older.

Cheltenham College was started as a business – a joint stock company in which each share carried the right to nominate a pupil. Situated in a fashionable spa town which was already notorious as a haunt of Anglo-Indians ('the remnants of whose livers sent them to drink the waters', commented Leach, the Victorian school historian, unkindly) it was focused firmly on that type of clientele and refused to have the children of tradesmen. 'Had we admitted tradesmen in the first instance,' wrote the secretary to his opposite number at Brighton College, 'we must have done so almost without limit, and in the confined circle of shops in Cheltenham we should have had the sons of gentlemen shaking hands with schoolfellows behind the counter.'

Nothing could be franker than that, yet by following these criteria Cheltenham developed rapidly, with a yearly intake that rarely fell below a hundred. Of more consequence than this calculated snobbishness was the new role in education it pursued. Facing the fact that some of its sons would have to earn a living, Cheltenham set up a curriculum aimed at the professions acceptable to its clients; the Army, the Civil Service, and, to a lesser extent, the Church and the Law. The timetable for the higher forms was therefore guided as much by the examinations at Woolwich and Sandhurst as those of the universities. As Bamford remarks, half the school was conceived in the classical mould of Eton or Harrow, and the other half geared to do a job of work. ' The sceptics sneered at the vocational side, but it would require a mind totally deadened by tradition to deny some romance and cultural value to this "military and civil side" when we read the following: Extras – Sanscrit, Hindustani and Persian languages . . . '

Marlborough was another proprietary school, with shares offered at £50 each. It was originated by an enterprising clergyman, conveniently near the new railway junction at Swindon, with the notion of creating a national boarding school modelled on the 'seven' but cheaper. In their anxiety to attract the children of clergymen, the governors set the fee too low (£30 a year for them, £50 for laymen) with the result that parsons' sons poured in – 200 on the first day, 500 by 1848. According to the school's earliest historian, Bradley, the result was catastrophic. During its first ten years Marlborough was more like a prison than an educational establishment (as a matter of fact, the same architect went on to design Wormwood Scrubs). The seething mass of boys was packed into extensions to the original house, with nine forms crammed into the Upper School Hall. They were ruled with ferocious severity – the canes being ' weapons of hideous length and terrible circumference'.

Inevitably there was trouble, in the shape of a mutiny carefully timed to take place on 5 November 1851. Fireworks shot from every building, and a barrel of gunpowder exploded behind the headmaster's back. For two or three days there was chaos. The place echoed to ceaseless detonations; smoke drifted through smashed windows. After a week the head gave in and retired to a parsonage at Market Lavington, whereupon Dr Cotton arrived from Rugby to knock the new school speedily and efficiently into shape.

Wellington was unusual, since it was founded as a national memorial to the Iron Duke, who died on 14 September 1852. Enormous sums were expected to be raised from a public appeal, and though the Duke's family would have preferred to see bronze statues erected in every town, the Queen and Prince Consort had other ideas. They were in favour of a college devoted to the free education of officers' orphans.

However, despite tremendous publicity, a compulsory levy of a day's pay from all ranks of the army, and over a hundred thousand begging letters, only £105,000 was collected, and only a meagre £5000 more when the appeal was repeated. Since this was far short of what was needed, the project would probably have been dropped had not the Queen, the Consort and the Prime Minister thrown all their influence behind it. As it was, the redoubtable headmaster, Benson, quickly turned the place from a glorified orphanage into a major public school.

But the fervour for creating new public schools was most apparent in the ambitions of Nathanael Woodard, who was not content to found only one, but aimed at establishing a whole system of boarding schools. Woodard's idea was that they should be 'cells' of influence

– religious brotherhoods in fact – designed to regenerate Anglicanism in England. Speaking of 'the new army of the middle classes', he proposed to divide his schools into three grades on class lines. The top grade was for the rich, the sons of gentlemen, professional people and the clergy. The next was for farmers and prosperous tradesmen; while the bottom grade was dedicated to educating small tradesmen and artisans. The profits from the top-grade schools would serve to underwrite the others. (Woodard, who had been privately educated himself, happily based his budget for the lower schools on the diet sheet of the London Orphan Asylum.)

This grandiose project started quite humbly with a small establishment in Woodard's vicarage at New Shoreham, outside Brighton, in 1848. The religious aspect was already apparent in its name, SS. Mary and Nicholas Grammar School. The following year he founded Hurstpierpoint, and then Ardingly in 1858, when the original school was moved to Lancing. With a chapel the size of a cathedral, Lancing was the mother school, the centre of an empire that expanded to include Bloxham, Denstone, Ellesmere, Worksop and King's School, Taunton (a proprietary school with some useful sixteenth-century endowments which he bought for a song in 1880). Perhaps the secret of Woodard's success was the ability to combine a pastoral ethos with a financial ability to coax pennies out of a beggar's cap. By the time he died in 1891, the Woodard Corporation had raised half a million pounds, which was invested in eight boarding schools for boys and three girls' schools – one at Bognor, two in the Midlands.

But the cheeseparing tactics that this brilliant religious entrepreneur adopted to remain solvent, and indeed the low fees themselves, tended to deter the better-off clientèle for whom Lancing was designed to cater. Though Lancing described itself as being ' for the sons of clergymen and noblemen of limited means', it clearly could not educate them properly at £30 a year for board and tuition. Within a few years the fees went up to £58 and Lancing set its sights somewhat higher: now it was 'for the sons of noblemen, clergymen, professional men and others'. By the turn of the century the fees had reached a basic £73 and often more. But though there were some 120 boarders the school was far from full, and the proportion of upper-class parents still small. Despite its magnificent buildings, Lancing was not yet recognised as being a public school. 'This failure to attract sufficient pupils', wrote an old boy of the school, 'was a reproach to Lancing for fifty years', and illustrated the problems of creating a top-class school from scratch. It couldn't be run on a shoe-string.

Clearly Woodard was more successful with his second and third level schools. Hurstpierpoint, charging 33 guineas, had 300 boys in the 1870s, and there were over 400 boarders at Ardingly, which cost less than half that amount. These two and indeed the whole community of schools he built up, had a high Anglican, even Anglo-Catholic tone (boys were encouraged to make sacramental confession), which reflected Woodard's view that religion and education were inseparable. They were designed to restore allegiance to the Church of England.

During Queen Victoria's reign a hundred or more schools were founded to meet the growing demand for a Christian education with public school trappings. Yet these foundations began to take place when the traditional schools were dwindling in size. Between 1830 and 1835 the yearly number of boys entering the 'seven', plus St Paul's, fell from 575 to 412, a decrease of almost thirty per cent. These venerable institutions were under a cloud; for forty years they had been subjected to fierce criticism, most of it justified. They were attacked for their brutality, unchecked bullying, insanitary discomfort, and the tyrannical pedantry that sought to confine education to a barrack square of classical grammar and syntax. Though often admired, they tended to be avoided by the new middle-class clientele, who preferred to send their sons elsewhere.

In simple terms, the attraction of the new foundations was that they seemed to offer the same advantages as the old unreformed schools – fine buildings in spacious grounds, a gentleman's education, the membership of an exclusive caste – without the scandalous disadvantages that ran counter to the rising tide of evangelical religion.

Since the century began, the prosperous middle classes had increased enormously; the number of lawyers and doctors had doubled; the clergy had increased from about 7,000 to 16,000. Consequently, the demand for high-grade education was booming, and like the corporate raiders of today, a host of ambitious young headmasters, scenting money and power, rushed to revive slumbering grammar schools in the hope that by erecting new buildings and improving tuition they would succed in upgrading them to public school status. Often, like Pears and Thring, they ran badly into debt and were faced with appalling difficulties.

But many of them succeeded. With the exception of the 'seven' (and they themselves were reformed after the Clarendon Commission) practically every one of our major public schools owes its character and *réclame* to the efforts of a dynamic Victorian headmaster. Each had its 'great' head: one thinks of Benson at Wellington, Pears at Repton, Lyon and Harper at Sherborne, Osborne at Rossall, Philpotts at Bedford, Hart at Sedbergh. Yet three men of very different temperaments stand out above the others because of their seminal influence on education and indeed the whole concept of public schools. These three, who follow each other in chronological succession, were Arnold of Rugby, Thring of Uppingham, and Sanderson of Oundle.

Dr Arnold is the most celebrated – and the most controversial – headmaster. Yet curiously enough his fame as a schoolmaster was largely posthumous. During his own lifetime he was better known as a theological and political propagandist, forever holding forth on such matters as the Oxford Movement, Unitarianism, or Trades Unions. He started an unsuccessful weekly newspaper, wrote his own Roman History (mainly to counteract Gibbon) and resigned from the Senate of London University because it refused to make scripture a compulsory subject.

Above all he was a masterful, theatrical personality, obsessed with the idea of wickedness.

'That ashy paleness and that awful frown were almost always the expression of deep ineffable scorn and indignation at the sight of vice and sin,' affirms his biographer, Stanley. For Arnold, sin meant laziness, deceit, cribbing, bullying, even breaking bounds, which were inspired, 'in plain English, by the Devil'. And so his first aim was to change the whole tone and spirit at Rugby, to crack down on the brutality and depravity. 'It is not necessary that this should be a school of three hundred or one hundred or of fifty boys,' he proclaimed, 'but it is necessary that it should be a school of Christian gentlemen.' He listed his ideals in a definite order: 'First, religious and moral principles; secondly, gentlemanly conduct; thirdly, intellectual ability'. Arnold made Chapel the centre of school life. He was a hypnotic preacher, and his sermons had an extraordinary impact on many of the boys. Thomas Hughes recalls

> . . . the tall valiant form, the kindling eye, the voice, now as soft as the low notes of a flute, now clear and stirring as the call of the light infantry bugle . . . the long lines of the young faces, rising tier above tier down the whole length of the chapel . . . We listened, as all boys in their moods will listen (ay, and men, too, for the matter of that) to a man whom we felt to be, with all his heart and soul and strength, striving against whatever was mean and unmanly and unrighteous in our little world.

He was not a great innovator. Though interested in scientific developments, he excluded science from the curriculum for fear that it might divert pupils' concentration from more important matters. However, he brought a new approach to the teaching of classics and ancient history. 'He was the first Englishman,' says Stanley, 'who drew attention in our public schools to the historical, political and philosophical value of the ancient writers, as distinct from the mere verbal criticism and elegant scholarship of the [eighteenth] century.'

Yet he did so for moral and religious motives, because in his view, history should be taught as the story of God's dealings with Man. The strength of his Evangelism showed through all his actions, leading him to concentrate his attention on the brightest boys and virtually ignore the others. To achieve his purpose, he cultivated the loyalty of the Sixth form. As prime targets of his moral fervour, the prefects became disciples who filtered his standards through the school, and later carried the same sense of piety and high moral tone to other establishments – Vaughan to Harrow, Cotton to Marlborough, Philpots to Bedford, Hart to Sedbergh, Percival to Clifton, and so forth. It was these devoted admirers, along with Stanley's *Life*, Hughes' *Tom Brown's Schooldays*, and his own celebrated son Matthew, who were the architects of Arnold's legendary fame.

He was only at Rugby from 1828 until his death in 1842 at the age of forty-four. But during these fourteen years he started a scholastic revolution. 'By introducing morals and religion into his scheme of education,' wrote Lytton Strachey some eighty years later, 'he altered the whole atmosphere of public school life. . . After Dr Arnold no public school could venture to ignore the virtues of respectability.'

64

Thring at Uppingham (left) was an educationalist in the modern sense; he believed, unlike Arnold at Rugby, that the ordinary boy, as well as the academically-minded, had the right to a good education. He also emphasised the importance of environment, music and games.

Though Arnold was a radical, he had no illusions about what would happen if the lower classes had their way. Coming from good middle class stock himself, he was convinced that only the new class of prosperous people who were pressing for power could defeat the two dangers he believed to be threatening English society: on the one hand the aristocratic *ancien régime* which opposed every attempt to raise the lower classes; on the other, the Jacobins who were determined to reduce everyone to the lowest level. Conscious that the sons of Birmingham manufacturers and Manchester merchants had to be trained as leaders, he called for a systematic effort to ensure that they were educated in accordance with his ideals, that is, as Christian gentlemen. And if to succeed he had to turn on the evangelical heat to an almost unbearable degree, he was going the right way to reassure anxious parents. Piety and high moral tone were precisely what the new customers wanted.

Arnold's concept of school as a place to train character became the aim of Victorian establishments. In short, his main achievement was to have inspired a new type of school for a new type of parent. The result, wrote Trevelyan, was that 'the old landed gentry, the professional men and the new industrialists were educated together, forming an enlarged and modernised aristocracy, sufficiently numerous to meet the needs of government and leadership in Victoria's England and Victoria's Empire'.

In some respects Thring was more of an innovator, for he was an educationalist in the modern sense, one of the first to be interested in method. Unlike Arnold, who concentrated his energy on the Sixth form and had no time for dunces, Thring believed that the ordinary boy had as much right to an education as his academically gifted fellow. The notion – shared by Sanderson – that every boy was good for something led him to expand Uppingham's curriculum quite radically. Pupils were taught the traditional fare in the morning, but in the afternoons they were allowed to study optional subjects such as modern languages, chemistry or drawing. He laid great emphasis on music (which at that time was considered to be an occupation for young ladies) and on improving the material environment, arguing that a large part of the 'moral miasma' which troubled Arnold resulted not so much from the devil as from squalid surroundings. External conditions, Thring insisted, affect character; and the fine buildings he erected were designed to bring out the best in masters and boys. On the moral side, too, it was not enough for the Sixth form to be responsible to him. The whole school should be responsible for itself.

Most of all, Thring preached the importance of physical training, and it was largely through games that he built up Uppingham's reputation, as we shall see later on. He was certainly a more attractive character than Arnold (for one thing, he had a sense of humour) and if he never achieved the same renown as his redoubtable predecessor at Rugby – though he founded the Headmasters' Conference – at least he has never been subjected to the same malicious reappraisal in the twentieth century. Perhaps Ogilvie, author of *The English Public School*, is right in suggesting that whereas Arnold reminds us of the Old Testament, Thring was of the New.

As for Sanderson – well he, of course, shall have a chapter to himself.

VII
A PERIOD OF TRANSITION
OUNDLE FROM SHILLIBEER TO STANSBURY

ON 9 JULY 1799 Thomas Bullen laid the foundation stone for a new building – now part of the east wing of the Cloisters – which symbolised the revival of Oundle's fortunes. On the surrounding masonry were inscribed the names of his sixty-seven pupils, though sadly some were lost or became illegible when windows were put into the wall a century later. No trace remains, for instance, of Chapman Marshall, a future Lord Mayor of London. But one can still decipher the inscription of Wynn Ellis, who became a wealthy silk merchant and bequeathed his collection of Old Masters to the National Gallery, as well as those of Major J.D.Bringhurst who died at Waterloo and H.James, whose brother was to become Bullen's successor.

Bullen's efforts to extend and give a scientific slant to the curriculum met with considerable success, as we saw. Oundle began to get a name for its practical tuition. At the same time it became more of a boarding school. From 1801 to the time of his resignation, Bullen admitted 143 boarders against a mere fifteen day-boys; indeed his successor found nothing but boarders. But the strain of accomplishing this revival overtaxed his strength, and when Thomas Dix left along with his brother James, Bullen had trouble finding assistants of their calibre. After a while as the burden of running the school became too great, his health broke down and in 1809 he resigned, only to die shortly afterwards.

To take his place, the governors appointed the Rev. John James, a fellow of St John's College, Oxford. He was the only properly qualified applicant. For his part James gave up his college fellowship and took to school mastering because he wanted to get married. The new headmaster (who later became Canon of Peterborough Cathedral) was above all a cleric, and since no documentary evidence exists to suggest a change of heart at Grocers' Hall, it must have been due to him that the brave new shift towards science and practical technology was quietly dropped from the curriculum. Such subjects were hardly to a classicist's taste. Nevertheless the school continued to prosper, though essentially as a country grammar school for the sons of squires, clergy, professional men and well-to-do farmers. There were very few free scholars at this time.

The overflow of boarders who could not be accommodated in the School House were lodged with private families around the town, or lived with the usher, as Lord Lilford's son did in 1813. In due course the usher (or 'Second Master' as he was now styled) opened a boarding house himself. John Shillibeer, who was second master towards the end of James' time, had ten boarders of his own when he took over as headmaster. All the same, the school's facilities were still very limited, which hampered any thoughts of expansion.

It also restricted the headmaster's income. The school year was divided into two halves, beginning on 1 February, and 1 September. Boarding fees were £42 a year, including tuition; the day-boys had their latin free, but had to pay for English, writing, and mathematics. In comparison with the Master of Oakham, who could take 70 boarders at 50 guineas, or even Uppingham's 50 at 40 guineas, James was at a distinct disadvantage. His salary barely covered the cost of a competent assistant, whose payment was his responsibility and the balance was hardly sufficient to pay the taxes on his house. He was therefore obliged to live on the profit he could make from the boarding fees (along with his stipend as curate of Oundle).

Consequently the handicap of cramped quarters must have been very much on James' mind. It was still impossible to expand around the schoolroom, and the boys had practically nowhere to play save the churchyard. So he turned an acquisitive eye in the opposite direction to the property that lay behind his house, that is, between Church Lane and the vicarage.

Gradually, with the help of two Old Oundelians and the support of a few far-sighted governors, it was acquired. First, William Walcot, who had been at the school under Murthwaite and was now an overseer, bought the building in Church Lane which was being used as a slaughterhouse, and passed it on at cost price. It wasn't very large, but at least this removed unpleasant smells from opposite the headmaster's study. Next, and more important-ly the White Hart inn, together with the horse-market which stretched through to the churchyard, came up for sale and were bought by John Smith, the brewer and banker, who as a boy had come to the school from Stoke Doyle in 1779. Smith offered these to the school at cost, on the understanding that he could lease back the public house for twenty-five years. Finally, through Walcot's intervention, the two properties immediately adjacent to the headmaster's house were secured as well as three cottages on the south side of Church Lane. Thus by the time James left, nearly all the site of the present cloister, and a good part of Church Lane too, were in the hands of the Company, though only half of this was available for immediate use by the school. If nothing else, John James prepared the ground for the school's subsequent expansion.

The Rev. John Shillibeer, who replaced him in 1829, was a member of the family which started the first London omnibus service in that year. But Shillibeer himself is chiefly remembered for his many sketches of the town, one of which is reproduced here.

He was also responsible for two exhibitions being granted annually from Oundle School to the universities. Appropriately, the first recipient, Frederick Yorke, later became the school's first historian.

Shillibeer's twelve years at Oundle corresponded roughly with those of Arnold at Rugby. But whereas his younger contemporary was busy making headlines and history, Shillibeer was content to maintain the status quo. In an era when many schools –including Rugby–

*Shillibeer, headmaster of Oundle from 1829-41, was also an artist. Above His 'Oundle Market Place'
(c.1826) shows the Town Hall then recently completed. To the left is today's School bookshop.*

found their intake falling, Shillibeer kept his numbers comfortably above the fifty mark.

However, the ratio of free scholars to boarders increased. In 1835 the day-boys numbered
22 out of a total of 57; in 1837, 27 out of 55. And this shift of balance brought complaints
over the charges that James had instituted for teaching writing and arithmetic. A good
classical education was provided free, in accordance with Laxton's endowment. But if
parents wanted their children to study additional subjects, they had to pay 6 guineas a year
– which was both a deterrent and a source of irritation.

Some of the local people spoke of petitioning the Company to provide a sound commercial education as freely as the existing classical one; others thought that the Governing
Body could be compelled to do so. Doubtless they had the case of Rugby in mind, where in
a somewhat similar situation the school trustees had been forced by legal action to expend
on the charity the total profits derived from Sheriff's legacy. It was the old argument that
because boarders were more profitable, the day-boys were neglected and advantages intended for them were enjoyed by boarders from outside.

The 1840 Act for improving and extending the benefit of grammar schools gave validity
to their grievance. But since Shillibeer was popular in the town, no action was taken out

of personal regard to him. However, in April 1841 Shillibeer suddenly died. After that, events moved quickly.

A petition bearing the signatures of 114 inhabitants, headed by the vicar, was sent to the Company. In sonorous, respectful language it requested that 'a more extended system of education be taught freely by adding a general course of English to that of a classical education'. In other words, 'please do away with those 6 guineas a year'.

Unfortunately certain other inhabitants went further and presented a Petition to the Lord Chancellor. Whereupon the governors, who might otherwise have taken a sympathetic view of the request, refused to negotiate under threat. Consequently the matter went to law. In the meantime the second master, David Pooley, was promoted headmaster.

The petitioners in the lawsuit that took place two years later did not ask that the school should lose its character as a grammar school by becoming an elementary school, although under the Act of 1840 that was possible. What they desired was that the boys of the Foundation – that is those resident in the town of Oundle – should receive the whole of their school education freely. Misled, perhaps, by the Rugby case, they felt that Laxton had intended the whole proceeds of his London estate to be devoted to the support of the school and the almshouses. In substance they believed that the Grocers could be convicted of misappropriation, and compelled to introduce free commercial education.

The case, which came up before the Master of the Rolls, Lord Langdale, who had previously given judgement on the Rugby affair, failed. The arguments between learned counsel for both sides were lengthy, and showed how difficult it was to interpret a deathbed will made nearly three centuries earlier – or indeed to make a will that would hold for so long. However, stressing the point that the codicil was a result of discussion, and a record of agreement with the Wardens of the Company, Lord Langdale ruled that the devise to the Company was a devise on condition. It did not make the Grocers trustees, for it was intended to be beneficial to the Company. It bound the Company to the minimum payments with which it was charged, now amounting to more than double the figures mentioned in the codicil. The case was therefore dismissed. Nor did Langdale accept an attack on the boarders. The Orders showed that they had been anticipated from the start; and undoubtedly the day-boys gained by sharing instruction that was good enough to attract those boarders.

So that was that. The whole business was 'foolish and vexatious from start to finish', wrote John Smith (who had opposed it all along). Nevertheless, it caused a good deal of ill-feeling towards the Company which lingered on and influenced later events. One of Stansbury's chief tasks, after he took over in 1848 was to re-establish harmonious relations between the Company and the townspeople.

Meanwhile this acrimony affected the school's intake. Pooley's records show that of the seventy-five boys he admitted, only sixteen were day-boys – clearly a reversal of the previous trend. But the staple fare remained Latin and Greek. 'The Classics claimed rather more attention than the other subjects,' Pooley wrote shortly before his death from a stroke at the age of thirty-three. 'But English literature was by no means neglected, sufficient regard being paid to History, Geography, Arithmetic as well as to Modern Languages'. By this he meant that if the morning's work was devoted to the Classics, other subjects were taught in the afternoon – including French once a week from a visiting Parisian.

Certainly the timetable kept everyone busy. School hours were from seven to five-thirty, with three breaks for meals or a breather; Wednesdays and Saturdays were half-holidays. Prayers were held twice daily; on Sundays the boys attended church and received religious instruction both in the morning and in the evening. What's more, there was prep to be done out of school. Pupils had to present a piece of Greek or Latin composition every day.

The school was divided into five forms. The top form read Demosthenes and Juvenal; the Fourth read Virgil and Homer, the Third and Second Ovid and Greek *Delectus*, while the lowest form started with Eutropius and the Latin *Delectus*. They were all taught together in the old schoolroom. On dark winter days it was neither agreeable nor of any help that the tuition took place in a building which dated from 1485. In fact it was necessary to start the day with recitations and verbal instruction until the gloom dispersed sufficiently for reading to become possible. In the fading evening light it was, of course, the other way round. The headmaster and the second master took the top forms alternately, and the other three forms went in rotation between them and the junior or visiting teachers. Thus the two always heard the whole school, which was still, after all, quite small, and not yet, admittedly, of any great distinction.

But what you might call the dramatic action was about to hot up. With hindsight it can be seen that 1848, a momentous year in European history, was a watershed for Oundle too. And this because the advent of Dr Stansbury gave a new momentum which was to raise the school to prominence by the end of the century.

The Rev. John Fortunatus Stansbury (who was born in Calcutta in 1805) received his DD after graduating from Magdalen Hall, Oxford. He had been headmaster of Queen Elizabeth's Grammar School at Kingston-on-Thames for fifteen years at the time of his appointment to Oundle. Previous to that, while still a curate at Folkestone, he married Eliza Layton, whose brother James was a Grocer and one of the school's governors. The new headmaster was therefore in a better position than most to negotiate and gain concessions from the Company. He was also a good teacher: under him, the school began to expand and acquire a considerable reputation for classical and mathematical scholarship.

Dr Stansbury was not impressed by what he found on his arrival. The schoolroom was dark and chilly, the boys had no playground to speak of, there was no library. There were very few pupils either, for the Second Master, disappointed at not being promoted himself, had departed taking some of the boys with him, with the result that only 18 boarders and four day-boys presented themselves to the new Headmaster. Moreover, the animosity of the town was evident. 'I have much to contend with,' Stansbury wrote to the Company, 'perhaps

Stansbury, headmaster of Oundle from 1848, is seen (right) *in a photograph taken at the time of his retirement in 1876.*

more than the Court is aware of.' It was time for change he told them, to meet the requirements of the age.

When asked for his proposals, he suggested that the Company should pay the contentious six guineas a year itself as a capitation fee, and thus restore free education to the school. He thought that the masters' salaries should be augmented; that more exhibitions should be given; that a yearly grant should be made to build up the library. Significantly, he put forward the idea that there should be an Upper and a Lower school – one school for boys not going on to college, and another for those who wished to read higher classics and mathematics. These changes would cost a good deal of money, to be sure. But he knew that the income from the Laxton bequest had nearly tripled since the beginning of the century, and therefore the Grocers could afford to pay for them.

The Company did not act on his suggestion to divide the school for another twenty-five years. But in substance they adopted his other proposals, bearing in mind that elementary education provided by the British and the National schools in the town was not free, and that some charge had to be made to protect their interests. The new orders that were drawn up in June 1851 also limited the number of boarders the headmaster might take into his house, and precluded him from accepting any other duties as his predecessors had done.

What this meant to the local townspeople was that instead of paying an entrance fee of half a crown and six guineas a year, they would henceforth pay £1 entrance fee and £2 a year. For this their sons would be educated not only in Latin and Greek, but also in a range of subjects including Mathematics, English, French, History and Geography, as well as religious instruction. They would also have an increased number of university exhibitions open to them. If the limitation of boarders appeared to check any tendency of growth into a boarding school, in practice Oundle was still 'open to the world', that is, to all who wished to come and enter their names in the Register. After all, there was nothing to prevent the other masters from taking in boarders if they wished.

These new arrangements met with immediate success. A few months later the examiners reported that the school had trebled since their visit of the previous year, and declared that the increased facilities would be beneficial to the area. As the applications for admittance rose, Dr Stansbury sought leave to increase his number of boarders to thirty. The Second Master and the Commercial Masters also began to take in boarders, though these were counted as day-boys or Laxton scholars.

Not surprisingly the problem of the schoolroom now became acute. The Company's surveyor, Mr Gwilt (himself the editor of an architectural encyclopaedia), wanted to restore the old Tudor building 'which is in the simple style of the period and cannot be improved'. Unfortunately the governors thought otherwise: they decided that it should be replaced by a completely new building.

While this work was in progress, the school had to make do with rented accommodation in Albion House at the other end of the town. Nevertheless, numbers continued to rise. By the time the 1855 building was opened, there were 100 Laxton scholars and 30 boarders in the headmaster's house, a far higher number than great schools such as Westminster or Charterhouse, and a remarkable contrast to the empty benches of four years back.

To mark the opening of the new Schoolroom (which is now the headquarters of the Laxton School) Dr Stansbury introduced a college cap – adorned with a silk tassle for seniors – thus the first hint of uniform came into being. And on 30 August 1855 the first cricket match was played against Uppingham, which the visitors won by eight wickets.

Recording these events, the earliest edition of *The Oundle Gazette and Northampton Adviser* reported that the school had reopened under the care of six masters. Assisting Dr. Stansbury were H. Weightman for mathematics, F.Y. St Leger for Classics, Monsieur Brière from Paris for French, and Messrs Kingston and Featherstone as commercial masters (i.e. men who did not teach Classics and had no degree) for other subjects.

Weightman replaced the previous second master, Rev. W. Watson, who had left after a quarrel with the headmaster. St Leger later went to South Africa and became the owner of the *Cape Times*. But the most serious setback for Stansbury was to be caused by the two commercial masters.

The first intimation of trouble came when Watson retained his house after resigning, and withdrew all but one of his twelve boarders, whom he continued to teach. (As late as June 1872 the School XI played cricket against Rev. W. Watson's pupils, and beat them.) But the defection only a few months later of the two commercial masters had more serious effects, for Mr Featherstone had thirty-two boys and Mr Kingston twenty-two. Many of these boarders lived in Northampton, and after consultation with the boys' parents, the pair of them decided to resign and open a private school there. Abingdon House, as it was called, flourished for many years, and gained a considerable reputation for games.

The loss of so many boys reduced the number of Laxton scholars from 96 at midsummer to 46 the following half year. Throughout Oundle's history, as we have seen, the fluctuations in numbers had often been as sudden and unpredictable as in a game of snakes and ladders. But to be faced with such a drop was a crippling blow.

Dr Stansbury reacted to it by appointing his son Adolphus to the staff and giving him a boarding house. He did not intend to be caught out in the same way again. It was an uphill struggle, but after seven years he managed to reach the same attendance as before the desertions of 1856. Thomas Hare, an inspector for the Charity commission, reported that every seat in the large schoolroom was filled; the six masters and 132 boys working satisfactorily to all concerned, a striking contrast to the scathing comments made by the Commission about other endowed schools.

Indeed the Victorian County History of Northamptonshire thought that the report made by T.H. Green for the Endowed Schools Commission in 1866 'almost verged on enthusiasm'. (T.H. Green, it will be recalled, was a philosophy don at Oxford and a busy political figure, who retained happy memories of his time at Rugby and 'those most luxurious canoes in which one can paddle for hours without the least exertion and undisturbed by eights or such abominations'.) Praising what the governors and headmaster had achieved, he attributed Oundle's success to having been conducted on 'a rather peculiar system, and with results on the whole very satisfactory' which he thought other schools would do well to follow. But the manners of the boys struck him as being rough, and he drew a sharp distinction between the social class of the boarders and that of the Laxton scholars. 'It cannot be said' he concluded 'that the problem of combining the education of the classes, roughly distinguished as professional and commercial, has been solved here, for a parent of the former class, if at all fastidious, would not find the school quite what he wanted'. A typically mid-Victorian comment which was to have its impact later on.

Meanwhile in 1867 Dr Stansbury bought Christopher Swann's family, commercial and posting Inn, the Dolphin, and renamed it Dryden House (after the poet, who was born at Aldwincle and often stayed at Oundle on his way to and from Cotterstock Hall). To this building Stansbury moved his son's house. Subsequently he acquired two adjoining properties in West Street – part of what is now called Cottesmore – and in March 1869 Laxton House was opened there under the care of his sister, Miss Elizabeth Stansbury. Finally in October 1874 he purchased the adjoining Plough Inn as an extension for Laxton House.

In this way the headmaster kept the boarding houses in the hands of his family, though it was perhaps unwise to have allowed the school to take on the aspect of a family business at a time when there was intense local interest in the reform of middle class education in Northants.

To make matters worse, the 'uxorious old man' as he was described in a national newspaper, disposed of two wives in quick succession and married a third. By his second wife he had a son; the third wife had been a maid in his previous household. It should be explained that a year after the death of his first wife he married his sister Elizabeth's companion, Miss Morgan, who refused to live in Oundle and indeed instituted proceedings for maintenance before dying soon after the birth of their baby son (which did not survive either). But the arrival at School House of a third Mrs Stansbury caused tongues to wag and the press to suggest, quite unfairly, that he was not a fit person to be the headmaster of Oundle. (The gossip about the unfortunate Dr Stansbury may have given Anthony Trollope the idea for his novel, *Dr Whorple's School*, which he wrote at Thrapston only a year or two later.)

An outbreak of typhoid fever in the school also added to Stansbury's troubles. When faced by a similar problem at Uppingham, Thring solved it by moving the whole school to Borth for a year while the sanitary authorities put matters right. But Stansbury, who as a member of the Sanitary Board had for a long time been concerned in bringing more up to date sanitation to the town, chose to take less drastic action. After the Northants medical officer had threatened to close the school, Stansbury drew on his knowledge of drains and sewers, and set men to work on the school buildings. Then, bypassing the county authorities, he asked Gwilt, who was still the Company's surveyor, to check and confirm that the sanitary arrangements were satisfactory. Luckily there were no more outbreaks of disease. But a sense of uncertainty persisted, and numbers again began to dwindle.

These factors contributed towards the Governors' decision to buy up Stansbury's interest in the school and pension him off. Times were moving on; it was a period of transition. The need for change in an accelerating world was reluctantly being recognised and even if many of the developments they envisaged had been proposed by Stansbury himself, twenty-seven years at the job was sufficient. Clearly the old man was no longer a dynamic enough headmaster to cope with the wider reorganisation of the school that they had in mind. In 1876 he was replaced by Henry St John Reade, and a new era for Oundle began.

VIII
THE PENALTY OF SUCCESS
OUNDLE FROM READE TO MUNGO PARK

THE CLARENDON COMMISSION was set up in 1861, and spent three years investigating the inner workings of the Great Schools. Its findings provided a feast for the radical press, who were able to reveal, amongst other things, that the Provost and fellows of Eton were still milking the college of much of its revenues, and that at Westminster masters had no control over the monitors, who treated them with contempt. Westminster fags had to rise at three a.m. and be at the prefects' disposal for the rest of the day; failure to do so at the double was rewarded by having to stand with one foot in a washbasin and be kicked with especially heavy boots. Yet despite such startling disclosures the commission's conclusions were on the whole favourable. While recommending certain administrative reforms, the commissioners gave the existing system their stamp of approval:

> These schools have been the chief nurseries of our statesmen . . . In them men of every profession or career have been brought up on a footing of social equality and have contracted the most enduring friendships and some of the ruling habits of their lives; and they have perhaps the largest share in moulding the character of an English gentleman.
>
> *(Public Schools Inquiry 20. p56)*

The public schools did not prepare boys to engage in modern science and technology, the report noted. But this was a superficial defect which could be corrected by curricular adjustment. What counted was that they prepared boys as no other schools seemed to do to meet the 'eternal testing realities of human social intercourse'. They produced men who, on the whole, were resourceful and adaptable, calm under pressure, and practical in judgement.

This litany of self-congratulation was echoed by other influential voices. 'Boys under private tuition are preparing to live' declared William Johnson; 'in public schools they live'. Sir James Fitzjames Stephen thought that no other educational system was so healthy and bracing to the mind. A public school was 'a sort of grammar and dictionary of human nature'.

Yet in linking their praise to a recommendation for 'order and discipline', the Commissioners were preaching to the converted, for during the past twenty years the schools had been changing of their own accord. 'The manners of the great schools' remarked the *Quarterly Revue* 'have been greatly improved of late years by the softened tone of society at large'.

Fighting had gone out of fashion, to be replaced by organised games. Previously headmasters had taken little interest in such matters. Barrow, the head of Harrow, considered football to be a game fit only for butcherboys. When Moberly of Winchester spoke of 'idle boys', he meant boys playing cricket. Now it was the reverse. When Warre, who was to succeed Hornby as headmaster of Eton, alluded to 'idle boys' he meant boys who were *not* playing cricket, or some of the other approved games. The process of regimentation was already beginning, and with it came a spirit of Victorian prudery. As the century advanced, schoolmasters became obsessed with 'impurity'. (Montagu ordered boys' pockets to be sewn up at Harrow; Percival of Clifton required that their knees should be kept covered when playing football, and so forth.) All of which amounted to an increase in the autocratic control that grew up over every activity outside the classroom.

The corsetting of youthful spirits and worship of athleticism (as a substitute for less moral pursuits) would have occurred without any persuasion from the Clarendon Commissioners. It was in tune with the Victorian way of life. But the Commission did check some abuses and influence certain trends. Notably, one of its conclusions was that

> The teaching of natural science should, whenever practicable, include two main branches, the one comprising chemistry and physics, the other comparative physiology and natural history, both animal and vegetable. A scheme for regulating the teaching of the subjects should be framed by the Governing Body.

Eton took the hint by introducing physical science as a regular subject for the Fifth form in 1869, and for the Remove in 1875. But the battle of the subjects became more intense as a result of the Taunton Commission on Endowed Grammar Schools. Its proposals were put to Parliament and resulted in the Education Bill of 1869, which set up education commissions with powers to introduce the reforms they thought necessary.

The Clarendon Commission was concerned with the education of the upper classes; the Taunton Commission dealt with that of the middle classes – though some of the schools they investigated were destined, like Oundle, to join the higher ranks later on.

One problem was that of the endowments, which together amounted to a very large sum. If redistributed on a national scale, could they not form the financial basis for a national system of secondary education? Then again, there was the question of education and social class. How many types of school should there be, and what types of education were most suitable? The Commissioners concluded that:

> The wishes of the parents can best be defined in the first instance by the length of time during which they are able to keep their children under instruction . . . Education, as distinct from the direct preparation for employment, can at present be classified as that which is to stop at about 14, that which is to stop about 16, and that which is to continue till 18 or 19: and for convenience we shall term these the Third, the Second, and the First Grade of education respectively. The difference in the time assigned makes some difference in the very nature of the education itself.

In their opinion, parents of the first grade comprised the aristocracy, the gentry, professional men such as clergymen, doctors, lawyers, and prosperous businessmen. These people were conservative by nature, and equated education to social requirements. They put their faith in the classics, which were closely linked to the upper class. And this view was held by headmasters of the major schools, who ruthlessly screened their admissions, being well aware of the amount of social mixing that parents would tolerate.

Matthew Arnold, himself a school inspector, defined the problem thus: 'We have amongst us the spectacle of a middle class cut in two in a way unexampled anywhere else; of a professional class brought up on the first plane with fine and governing qualities, but without the idea of science; while that immense business class, which is becoming so important a power in all countries, on which the future so much depends, and which in the leading schools of other countries fills so large a place, is in England brought up on the second plane, cut off from the aristocracy and the professions, and without governing qualities.'

This was the dilemma that faced the Company's Oundle committee when it met to plan the reorganisation before appointing a new headmaster. Stansbury's suggestion that a more modern curriculum would give the school wider local support was reinforced by a petition submitted by the Northants Chamber of Agriculture, couched in these words:

> That whilst fully recognising the high position to which the Grammar School of Oundle has attained with regard to Classical and Mathematical education, this Chamber, seeing that the school is situated in the midst of a purely agricultural population, strongly urges upon the Grocers' Company the necessity of adding to the present subjects taught in the school the following, viz., Chemistry, Natural Science and Mechanical Drawing, as the education now given is not of such a nature as to meet the requirements of the present population.

Moreover the Endowed Schools Department was becoming involved in the matter. The Commission's secretary, Richmond, told J.H. Warner, a Warden of the Company, that he believed a First–grade Modern school should be created 'lest as a classical school it should clash with Uppingham, Stamford, and others close by'. To satisfy local demand for a lower grade school, he suggested that the Company should subsidise the Latham (or Blue Coat) school at Oundle.

Richmond thought, perhaps erroneously, that Warner was impressed with this idea. Yet the Grocers themselves were clearly divided over the character that the school should adopt. At a crucial meeting in November 1875, it was Joseph Warner who proposed that Oundle should become a First-grade Classical school with special facilities for teaching modern subjects, whereas Richard Hilhouse spoke for those who favoured turning it into a First-grade Modern school. This would certainly have cost more, but cost was not the decisive factor. The needs of the local boys had to be balanced against the necessity of making proper use of the boarding houses that were being acquired from Dr Stansbury. Here the recent recommendation by the Northants Education Board to make Oundle the Classical boarding school of the county (in apparent contradiction to the other authorities) must have weighed with the more conservative minded members of the committee. Yet curiously enough Dr Stansbury's compromise scheme to create a First-grade Classical school alongside a local Second-grade Modern school was not even mentioned.

In the final show of hands, Warner's Classical school was supported by eleven members, against ten in favour of Hilhouse's Modern school. Thus by a single vote Oundle's future was decided for the next seventeen years – though there were rumblings in the background.

The next step was the appointment of a new head. From thirty–four applications, the Governors chose a man with impeccable qualifications. Henry St John Reade came from an Oxfordshire family with a seat at Ipsden House, and was the nephew of Charles Reade, the novelist. At Tonbridge he had been head boy and the first captain of the Cricket XI, winning a scholarship in Classics at University College, Oxford, where he took a first in Honour Moderations and a second in Greats, and captained the Varsity Cricket team in 1862. Chosen to be one of the assistant masters on the founding of Haileybury College, he became one of the first housemasters, founded the literary society and instituted concerts, got the cricket going, and (rather as a ladder to success, one feels) was ordained by the Bishop of Rochester. After resigning his house to marry the granddaughter of Dean Vincent (the headmaster of Westminster who expelled Southey) he became headmaster of Fawl-kenberg at Beccles, a school roughly the same size as Oundle, and then the Godolphin School at Hammersmith.

Intensely ambitious, he seemed just the right man to give Oundle a lift. Of that there could be no doubt. But the speed with which he did so took everyone by surprise.

To a person of his background Oundle must have seemed somewhat old-fashioned. There were no compulsory games, no house matches, no Sixth form, no prefects, no tradition of Speech Days, no societies, no school magazine, no uniform apart from the college cap. At a time when bat and ball fever had already become a sort of religion, and the fortunes of the country seemed to rely on an unfailing supply of schoolboy games heroes, there were not even any colours at Oundle.

Reade changed all this overnight. During his first term – the summer term of 1876 – the top boys were appointed prefects (who read Latin précis during prayers); the Fifth form became the Sixth, complete with mortar boards; games were made compulsory; and to organise them better, early school before breakfast and three half-holidays a week were introduced. Twelve cricket matches were played that summer, with Reade taking part except in those against other schools.

Colours were awarded: the Cricket XI sported blazers with the Grocers' shield on the breast pocket, and blue caps with crest. On the last day of term glees and recitations (scenes from Molière and Canning's *Needy Knife-grinder* accompanied the prize-giving for swimming and diving. For Rugby football which followed in September, the First XV wore blue jerseys with the Grocers' emblem, white trousers with dark blue stockings pulled over them,

Reade (right) *was headmaster of Oundle from 1876-83. He oversaw the separation of the Classical and Modern Schools. The 'modern side' was to give 'a good and useful education to boys who leave school about the age of 16 in order to engage in Agriculture or Commercial pursuits'.*

and a black velvet fez adorned with a white silk tassel. The Second XV had the school shield on their house jerseys; the Third XV a red St George's cross. The distinguishing house colours were red and black for School House; light and dark blue for Dryden; blue and black for Laxton; and purple and white for Oppidans, as Reade called the day-boys. Though there was still no official school uniform, boys had to wear straw hats bearing their house colours. The day of the 'basher' had arrived.

Reade started his first term with 92 pupils – 32 day-boys and 59 boarders – including a few that he had brought with him from the Godolphin School. He knew exactly what he intended to do at Oundle, and he set out his programme to two of the governors, J.H.Warner and W.J.Thompson, when they visited the school early in June 1876.

Declaring that it was impossible to mix the two elements – pupils who were to study Classics and Mathematics and go on to the university, and those who would leave at sixteen and merely required elementary education – he told them that he had already begun a separation between the Classical and the Modern or rather between the First-grade and the

Second-grade schools, and they agreed to recommend this scheme to the Court.

A month later Reade explained his proposals to local parents at a meeting held in the Talbot. There would be a separate Second-grade school to accept boys from the age of nine and prepare them for the Cambridge Local Examinations, at a fee of two guineas a year plus eighteen shillings for books. It would open at Albion House in September and move into the Grammar School buildings when new ones had been erected for the Classical School. He added that he would make a point of teaching there himself, and would arrange for boys of ability to be transferred to the First-grade school. He also warned that there would inevitably be a social distinction between the boys of the two schools. Once again his scheme met with approval. It was unanimously considered that the middle class school would meet a long felt need in the town and neighbourhood

Thus the boys returned in September to find that there were now two schools: Oundle (as Reade named the Classical School, in his prospectus, quietly dropping the Grammar) and the Laxton Modern School 'to provide for the education of sons of tradesmen and farmers'. That, he felt, made things quite clear. The Company was to build new premises for the Classical School. and the Modern School would then occupy the present Grammar School buildings. The two together represented the original foundation, endowed by Sir William Laxton and placed by him under the Grocers as Governors. Similar divisions had taken place at Harrow and Bedford. It was a matter of common sense.

Unfortunately Reade was not a lawyer, nor a financier, nor a politician, nor a civil servant. What seemed simple to him appeared different to people who thrived on complexities. There were difficulties behind the scenes that he never suspected. Unbeknown to him, a storm was about to brew.

In the meantime, Oundle thrived as it had never done before. Numbers rose steadily to 217 in 1882. The first issue of the *Laxtonian* appeared in December 1876, and two months later the newly formed School Choral Society gave concerts in aid of the local benevolent fund. Reade created a carpenter's shop and made accommodation available for practical work in chemistry and experimental physics. Scientific apparatus was acquired for Mechanics, Botany, Geology, Astronomy and Physical Geography. Trophies were instituted for the Cock-House in rugger, athletics, and cricket. There were paper-chases when the playing fields became waterlogged, and when the floods froze time-off was allowed for skating or sliding on the ice. At Christmas there were theatricals performed by the Dramatic Society.

Those members of the governing committee who spent a week-end at Oundle in February 1879 were surprised at the importance the school had assumed. Not only did they endorse the plan to build a new range of classrooms for the Classical School at a cost of some £30,000, but in addition they recommended buying thirty acres of land to the north of Milton Road for £4,500. Mr Gwilt's designs for the Cloisters, as they are now called, were for a quadrangle with the old school house to the east and classrooms to the west; the other sides were to contain the Great Hall, library, museum and laboratory. A year later the Court unanimously gave the go-ahead to start building the classrooms. Early in November 1880 the demolition of the White Hart complex began. In cap and gown, Reade mounted a ladder to make a ceremonious beginning, and for a few delirious minutes the schoolboys were allowed to take part in the work of destruction.

After five years in office, the headmaster could feel confident that his policy was succeeding. Indeed the Report by the Oxford and Cambridge Examination Board had endorsed it in glowing terms.

Noting that numbers had grown 'to a point never previously approached', the examiners approved of the elimination of a lower-class element from the Upper school. It was now 'a First-grade public school composed exclusively of sons of gentlemen, almost all being boarders. This judicious separation of classes by the present headmaster has proved a decided success'. They were enthusiastic about the excellent classical work achieved by his Second Master, Robert Brereton. They had high praise, too, for Francis Sutton's efforts at the Modern School, declaring that it answered its purpose and that some of the boys came considerable distances each day to attend it.

These commendations were borne out by the brilliant stream of scholarships won during the previous year. Word was getting round that the school provided a good and inexpensive education for the sons of professional men; indeed sixty per cent of the boarders were sons of clergymen. As Reade's naval brother wrote: 'Oundle is getting its name up'. Speech Day in July 1881 was a splendid affair, with the Master and Wardens arrayed in their traditional robes. Declaring in his speech that the Governors had full confidence in the present management of the school, the Master voiced their determination to maintain and increase its prosperity.

Fine words. So what went wrong? For one thing, not all the Court agreed with the Master's sentiments. Some of them had begun to feel that Reade was less intent in developing a cheap school for poor men's sons than in making a great public school like Rugby or Uppingham, and this at their expense. They became increasingly suspicious of his ambitions for the future (just as both Arnold's and Thring's Governors had once been) particularly in the light of discussions that were going on with the Endowed Schools authorities. The trouble was that Reade appeared to know what he wanted to make of the school, whereas the governing body did not know its own mind. And they objected to being pressured into action.

At this point Reade made two unfortunate blunders. In January 1882 the Oundle committee began planning a readjustment of the terms on which the Company supported the school. Apart from considering the question of capitulations (since the ceiling of 200 boys had been passed) there was also a suggestion of raising the tuition fees. Consequently a letter was sent to the headmaster advising him that an accountant would be coming to prepare a detailed analysis of the school's financial affairs. For some reason it caught him on the raw and, without waiting to cool down, he replied by return of post objecting to 'this inquisitorial investigation' and referring the accountant to the statements already in the hands of the Court. It was hardly the sort of letter to write to businessmen of all people, but Reade was inclined to react hastily against any proposal he did not like at first sight.

To make matters worse, he felt that it was his duty to warn town parents who were intending to send their sons to the Classical School – the only ones who would be affected – that the fees were likely to go up.

He would have done better to keep this to himself, for word immediately spread that Sir William Laxton's cherished endowment was about to be withdrawn. A protest meeting was held in the Town Hall at which Reade was shouted down and a number of intemperate remarks were made. To townspeople the success of the Classical School was clearly a matter of indifference compared with a good and almost free education for their children. Indeed they objected to the social distinction between the two schools, which in their opinion benefited the headmaster and the Company, not themselves.

It was decided to draw up a petition, which would be taken by a delegation to the Grocers. Reade then issued an angry handbill (a favourite dodge in those days) refuting the allegations that had been made and advising people not to listen to false reports.

This was fatal to Reade. Greatly affronted at the turn of events – nothing, they felt, could have been in worse taste or more unworthy of a headmaster than the handbill – the Court passed a vote of non-confidence and requested his resignation.

Reade's reply, a letter covering eight foolscap pages, reveals his shock and surprise: he had obviously no idea how much he had fallen from grace. Of the four reasons for dismissing a headmaster – immorality, dishonesty, incompetence or disagreeableness – he concluded that in his case it must be the last. He asked the Court to reconsider. But they would not budge from their decision.

Commenting much later on this unhappy affair, Brereton, his devoted Second Master, said he thought that Reade had been in too great a hurry; under him the school had expanded too quickly and outgrown its facilities. This may have been a tactful way of implying that Reade had over-reached himself in trying to create a 'great school' under the noses of the governors. However, the clue to the matter is probably to be found in certain documents at the Public Record Office, notably those dealing with the proceedings of the Livery Companies Commission.

It will be remembered that the Grocers consulted the Endowed Schools Commission about their position at Oundle in 1876, but did not follow Richmond's recommendations. They subsequently enquired whether the consent of the Commissioners was necessary should they wish to make any material alteration to the buildings, and were advised that this was requisite under the Act of 1869. No scheme was put up; there was no official acceptance. Moreover when the Grocers thought it wise to obtain a licence from the Crown to confirm their title to what had already been bought – Dryden House, Laxton House, the properties in Church and New Streets – the Attorney-General declared that any property

The faded contemporary photograph (above) *shows the triumphal arch erected by the town on the occasion of the opening of the School Cloisters in 1883. The legend on the opposite side of the arch was:* 'Success to Oundle School'.

acquired without licence had become forfeit to the Crown. For some time, therefore, the Company must have been embarrassingly aware that its decisions to divide the school and spend munificently without the consent of the Charity Commissioners were, strictly speaking, illegal.

Now the proceedings of the Livery Companies Commission were largely a continuation of the campaign against the patronage and privileges of closed corporations started by Hobhouse and Roby in 1869. And their minutes of evidence dated 23 March 1882 were critical of certain City Companies' charities. Coinciding as it did with the uproar at Oundle, this damaging criticism must have influenced the Court's attitude towards Reade far more than the indiscreet way in which he had handled the trouble there. That simply provided the excuse for his dismissal. No, to put their house in order, the Grocers needed a scapegoat. Since no official action was ever taken against the Company for the obvious irregularities in its attempts to reform the school on its own, the conclusion is clear: the price of Reade's success was to be offered up as a sacrificial lamb.

No one can judge what he might have done at Oundle had he been allowed to stay on, as he had hoped, for a further ten years. He might have become one of the great headmasters. As it was, he died of cancer, not long afterwards. Yet in historical perspective it can be argued that his dismissal set off a chain of events which culminated in the appointment of Sanderson. And in the words of David Allsobrook (to whom I am indebted for some of the foregoing facts) the development of Oundle during Sanderson's headmastership was one of the most significant episodes, not only in the evolution of public schools, but in the history of secondary schooling in England and Wales.

For after Reade left, the school vegetated and declined.

Under the two successive heads, numbers fell to barely 100, despite the magnificent new classrooms and a fine new building opposite them for the School House, which was opened in 1887. Indeed in the golden age of public schools Oundle slumped so badly that it did not even feature in the *Public Schools Year Book* of 1889. For a full decade the Grocers were undecided on what course to take, vacillating between decisions to amalgamate the two schools into one, or to continue them separately. Finally they took the positive step, influenced perhaps by a report made for the Charity Commission by the Hon. W.N. Bruce, of transforming Oundle into a top-grade Modern School. Even so, it was a close run thing. Sanderson was only elected by the majority of a single vote among the twenty-nine members of the court.

But this was still ten years ahead. In the meantime, for the sake of appearances, it was agreed that Reade should stay on as head until the end of the summer term of 1883. And a trying time this must have been for him. When his resignation was announced, there was a feeling of dismay. A number of well-meaning parents wrote asking him to stay on at Oundle. He could well have taken advantage of the situation and moved elsewhere with their sons and some of his staff. Instead he soldiered loyally on, still playing cricket and even writing a play for the Christmas dramatics. One of his last acts was to supervise the formation of the Old Oundelian Club in 1883.

In April the Court enquired about a rumour that a boy named Bayley had been expelled for having climbed the church spire. Reade replied that the boy had not been expelled, but flogged for acting in defiance of a warning not to make the attempt. The exploit had been mentioned in the *Laxtonian* three years previously. (Indeed one of the Oundle legends is that, apparently in response to a challenge made by Captain Webb, the channel swimmer, Bayley scaled the steeple of St Peter's – 196 feet, the highest in the county – and tied his cap to the weathercock. It was said that after flogging him, the Head gave Bayley a guinea as a reward for his bravery.)

Now the matter was revived as an example of the lax discipline under Reade. By Victorian standards, there may have been some truth in this. H.D. Leigh, one of his most distinguished pupils, wrote after his old headmaster's death that 'Reade's aim was to create not a system, but a spirit and a character. The unique characteristics of Oundle were its happy life, the pleasant relations of teacher and taught, and comparative freedom. This idea could only be carried out by its author, and even in his hands its defects soon became apparent. It depended too much on the personality of the man and the co-operation of the boys.' (An example of the Oundle spirit was shown by Leigh himself, who concocted a letter to the *Standard* signed "Head Boy", suggesting that as the Head Masters' Conference had proved beneficial, so also might a Head Boys' conference be useful. The newspaper not only published the letter, but gave it a leading article as well.)

Humorous and independent, if you like, this spirit remains part of the Oundle ethos. But it was to be severely tried under the next headmaster, who was chiefly concerned with the state of Oundle's morals. Before he took over, Reade had assured him that all was well with the moral tone of the school. But the very next day Reade was advised of some sexual misdemeanours involving six boys in Dryden. Horrified, he wrote to the Court detailing the discovery and punishment of the boys who were concerned. However his successor considered that his own worst fears had been justified.

The Rev. T.C. Fry, a bald and pugnacious little man with whiskers as luxuriant as the hairy Ainu – though he came from Cheltenham, not Siberia – made such heavy weather of the affair because he completely misunderstood the character of the school. Attributing the trouble to lack of supervision in the overcrowded houses, Fry determined to correct it by insisting on the presence of masters everywhere, and started the practice of having assistant masters boarding in each house. He also reduced the numbers of boys in them by transferring the overflow to Sidney, which had been opened the previous January by Reade.

In his first week, the new Head drew up a list of draconian house rules:

1 No study door shall on any pretence be locked.
2 No non-study boy shall visit a study; and in a House where there are Junior studies, no Junior study boy shall visit a Senior study, except when sent for officially by the Senior Prefect of the House.
3 No boy except a Prefect shall leave his study or work room during the Evening work without leave from a master or from the Prefect in charge.
4 A boy from one House shall not be allowed to visit a boy in another House without distinct leave given on each occasion by the House Master. Prefects may visit Prefects.
5 No boy is allowed to go to any Dormitory but his own on any pretence whatever, except on duty authorised by his House Master.
6 During prayers in Dormitory, after the gas is out, silence shall be observed in every Dormitory: before gas is out and in the morning talking must be quiet, and general order strictly kept.

Abolition of freedom was Fry's remedy. Thus on learning that boys were going down to the level crossing to watch the trains, he forbade them to do so for fear of infection from

(Left) *The Rev. T.C. Fry's shortlived headmastership (1883-1884) is remembered for his attempt to impose draconian rules on School life so as to counter what he saw as the 'moral laxity' of the School as he found it.*

passengers alighting at the station. Thus certain seats in church had to be occupied by masters to keep watch on the boys' behaviour. A week-end exeat was granted at half term; but since it interfered with the work, this too was stopped. Old Boys were discouraged from visiting the school. Masters were confined to their common-room when they had a free period. The Literary and Dramatic societies died; cricket and rugger matches against other schools ceased.

And then, having put everyone's back up and established a sort of Victorian monolith, he suddenly resigned at the end of a year on grounds of ill-health. 'Over anxious to reform and over hasty in introducing a perhaps necessary but certainly alien system, he spoiled what would have been first rate work by annoying the Old Boys, irritating the staff, and rubbing boys up the wrong way. A good teacher and organiser, he had to deal with a situation that required tact and patience, and failed'. Such was an Old Oundelian's comment. Perhaps Fry learnt from his experience at Oundle, because he later achieved success as headmaster of Berkhamstead, and ended up as Dean of Lincoln.

The Rev. Mungo Park, a relative of the African explorer, took over as Head. After taking a Second in Greats at Lincoln College, Oxford, he had taught at Sherborne and been headmaster of the King Edward VI School at Louth. In contrast to Fry, he was a civilised man: scenes from *Henry IV, Part 2*, Molière's *Le Médecin Malgré Lui* and *The Frogs* of Aristophanes were enacted on the lawn at Cobthorne for his first Speech Day. But unfortunately he was indolent and ineffectual.

During his time the Boat Club was formed and two fives courts were built in the Cloisters. A house at the junction of the Stoke Doyle road, in which Cromwell was supposed to have slept in 1642, was acquired for Sidney (and among other things fitted with some handsome mahogany doors bought at a sale of effects during the alterations at Buckingham Palace). The new School House was opened. But in spite of having some of the best buildings in England, good teaching, and a list of university successes well above the average of other schools, Oundle slumped. Perhaps there remained an aura of unattractiveness about the place as a legacy from Fry: perhaps it was because the momentum had been lost, the incisive thrust blunted. As it was, while other schools thrived, Oundle was only held together by Brereton's brilliant scholarship. But since there was no provision for those who did not take kindly to the Classics, they departed. For though boys came, more left. Mungo Park started with 153 boys, but the numbers steadily fell – to 126 in 1887, to 104 in 1901. When Sanderson arrived, he found only 92.

Clearly by that time Oundle was no longer fulfilling any particular purpose. But as its long history attests, the moment that a new start was made to meet a definite educational need, the school began to flourish. And this was about to happen dramatically.

IX

SANDERSON AND THE GREAT LEAP FORWARD

During the early part of Queen Victoria's reign, a certain Lord Boyne lived on a large estate at a small village in Durham (wrote Lord Hemingford [the Hon. D.G.R. Herbert, Bramston, 1917-22]). On his estate was a labourer named Sanderson. This labourer and his wife had several sons, but one after another they died in early youth. One however, named Frederick William, lived. He went to the little village school, and on leaving, became a pupil teacher in another village school near by. The Lord of the estate and the local clergyman noticed that this student-teacher was a clever youth, and they encouraged him to try and get a scholarship to Durham University, promising to pay his expenses there. He got the scholarship and studied Theology and Mathematics with such success that he became a Fellow at the University.

He also gained an Open Mathematics scholarship at Christ's College, Cambridge, where he worked at Mathematics and Natural Science, hoping to get a Fellowship at Cambridge too.

He did quite well, but disappointed his friends and himself by failing to get the Fellowship. He had never failed in anything before, and he was now disheartened and miserable.

'Long afterwards, when I was at Oundle, I too twice failed in attempts to win a scholarship to Oxford, and he told me of his own bitter disappointment', recalls Herbert. 'You will learn that failure is often as valuable as success', replied Sanderson.

As it turned out Sanderson's failure was certainly of the greatest value, for after a few years of restless teaching work in Cambridge, he abandoned university teaching and started his career as a schoolmaster. At the age of 28 he became Senior Physics Master at Dulwich College, and here he found the work he loved.

In 1892 Oundle needed a new headmaster. It had been, notably in the time of Cromwell, a great school. But it had declined to only 92 boys. The governors were divided. Some thought they should continue the classical tradition of the school, others that they should introduce science and engineering. The latter won, and Sanderson was appointed Headmaster of Oundle by a majority of one vote.

He was appointed to reorganise and rejuvenate the school. But the staff and the boys disliked the idea of reorganisation and were determined not be rejuvenated. Nearly half the governors, most of the staff, and all the boys were bitterly opposed to the new headmaster. He was despised because he had not been educated at a public school himself, and was no athlete. He was distrusted because he was not, like previous headmasters, a clergyman. The school was used to a quiet, dignified head who seldom interfered in the ordinary routine of work. They now had a young energetic man who was determined to interfere in everything and change most things.

Every morning as the boys trooped into school Sanderson was there, watch in hand, to see if anyone was late. Every morning at prayers most of the school kept their mouths shut while the little boys sang the hymns. The Head ordered even the prefects to sing, just like the new boys – a thing they had never done before. He would explode with anger and furiously beat boys, some strokes of the cane falling on their arms and legs as well as the usual place.

He proceeded to reorganise the school in a highly unpopular way. On his arrival he found seven forms, each doing the same subjects – Latin, Greek, Mathematics, and French. In some of the forms there were a few odd boys who did Science and some who did German instead of Greek. Nobody bothered very much about those who did Science and German: staff and school looked on these subjects as inferior.

Sanderson at once divided the school into a Classical side and a Modern side. Boys who had been low down in the old forms were put into forms on the modern side, which ranked equally with the Classical forms. This greatly annoyed the majority who were on the Classical side. It was also disliked by the staff who had to do much more work now that there were more forms in the school. And almost everybody, masters and boys, was horrified at the sight of a headmaster taking personal charge of the teaching of the inferior science subjects.

Few headmasters can have been hated as thoroughly as Sanderson was.

The School Debating Society arranged a mock trial. The prisoner was a man who was supposed to have burnt down the science laboratories and the engineering workshops. The play was carefully written, and filled with insults to the new headmaster. For two or three weeks it was painstakingly rehearsed, with the approval of the staff. On the evening of the dress rehearsal the headmaster walked in. He sat down and listened. He never stopped the trial or interrupted it. When it was over there was a pause, everyone wondering what he would do.

He slowly rose, and said: 'Boys, we will regard this as the final performance,' and then walked quietly from the room. No interference, no argument, no anger. Only an extremely uncomfortable silence, leaving the boys surprised and disappointed, and a little bit ashamed.

For seven years Sanderson fought the opposition of the governors, masters, parents and boys. One night he sat down in his study, sick and tired and hopeless, and wrote out his resignation. He took the letter to the post office, but he never posted it. Through his head ran the words of *Isaiah*: 'They that wait upon the Lord shall renew their strength, they shall mount up with wings as eagles, they shall run and not be weary, they shall walk and not faint.' He tore the letter up.

However at the end of seven years he had won a complete victory. The boys had grown to respect him. He might do things they did not like, but he was a delightful teacher, and a most amusing man with a great sense of humour. There was something very attractive about him, if you treated him properly.

The old hostile masters were gradually replaced by men whom Sanderson chose. New boys came, who had never known the slackness and prejudices of the old Oundle. And the numbers of the school had increased by fifty. A workshop, laboratories and two new houses had been

F.W. Sanderson (left), headmaster from 1892-1922, was an inspired educationalist. Under him the School developed in leaps and bounds. The curriculum widened to include Science and Engineering, and to allow each boy to develop his own talents. New labs, workshops and classrooms were built; societies and sports were revived. H.G. Wells wrote: 'the Oundle of his later years was a brilliant success.'

built. The Science side was going ahead; the classical work had not suffered. The Literary Society had been started again; a photographic club had been established; a gymnastic class had been begun. There was more life in the school.

From that time onwards Sanderson never believed in the possibility of failure. If he were told that something was impossible, he replied: 'Things are only impossible, because people think they are'. And from that time on the school progressed in leaps and bounds.

Six new houses were opened. An Officers' Training Corps was formed. The acting of plays was introduced. A choral society and an orchestra were founded. A farm was started. A large science block, an assembly hall, a library and an art room were built. New playing fields were levelled, a gymnasium, a cricket pavilion and a boat-house appeared. A forge and a foundry were erected.

By 1908 there were 300 boys in the school, by 1917 there were 400, by 1922 there were 550,

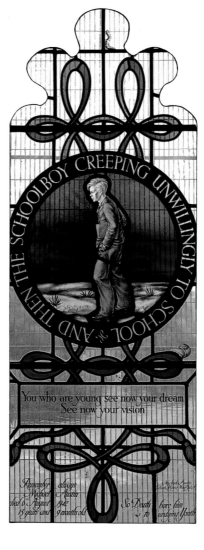

Previous page *The central panel of John Piper's three stained glass windows in the Chapel has three life-size figures of Christ, symbolising the Vine (a cup), the Bread of Heaven (a wafer) and the Water of Baptism and Regeneration (a bowl). The seven ambulatory windows in the Chapel, representing the Seven Ages of Man (the 'School boy is seen right) were designed by Hugh Easton and dedicated in 1950.*

The School Register (bottom left) is one of the oldest of any English school; it dates from 1626. The School's Frobenius organ (bottom right) was installed in 1984. Each year since the School has hosted the Oundle International Organ Week.

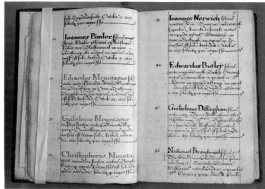

Right *The School Cloisters at night.* Bottom right *Today's sports facilities include sailing on the River Nene.* Bottom left *Creative work in the Music Department's electronics laboratory.*

Spectacular expeditions have become a feature of School life. The 1982 mountaineering expedition to China was the first such expedition to that country; the team ascended two 20,000 ft peaks near Mt Kongur (above). In 1983 another group visited Papua, New Guinea, climbing Mt Wilhelm (left). Far left The expeditioners try out native national costume.

worshipped sport he was suspected of attaching little importance to games. His politics were Liberal, if not Radical – he was a great admirer of Ruskin – and he was increasingly concerned with the improvement of the working classes. His badly tailored clothes, huge owlish spectacles, and north country speech were fair game for boys accustomed to making fun of a 'stinks beak'. He had a violent temper, which often flew out of control. But above all he was a worker, ablaze with a passion for toil. He expected, indeed demanded, that both staff and boys should show the same devotion to hard work and long hours – which was not to their taste. They felt that he was no sportsman, no cricketer, no scholar, no clergyman, no gentleman. And so from no quarter did he receive any welcome. Even the county society stood sniffily aloof.

For his part Sanderson immediately showed his intentions by bringing a scientist, H.O. Hale, from Cambridge, as Second Master, along with four Dulwich boys to complete their scientific education. (Their presence did nothing to improve his popularity.) He threw out the old scientific equipment and remodelled Bullen's 1799 building into Physics and Chemical laboratories. The former dining hall in Church Lane was converted into metal and wood workshops equipped with vices, lathes and carpenter's benches. The old smithy was cleaned out; a new forge was built, and a brass furnace installed.

The School itself was reorganised into four Classical, four Modern Languages, and four Science and Engineering forms, which were jointly arranged into nine mathematical sets. The Classical side continued with its normal curriculum. But the Modern Languages side aimed at preparing boys for the Army, Civil Service, or business careers; whereas the Science side set its sights on university scholarships in Natural Science, the London Inter-BSc. and Medical Preliminary examinations. The Engineering side dealt with those intending to go in for Civil, Mechanical or Electrical engineering, industry and agriculture. It was an

The School forge, seen left in a photograph of c.1921, was situated in a row of buildings and workshops adjoining the almshouses.

ambitious programme. Yet its thrust was clear: in Sanderson's words, 'ignorance of the uses of squared paper was evidence of a neglected education'.

He attributed the school's recent decline to an absence of discipline, a classics-soaked structure, and a dilatory staff. 'I have been surprised to find that the assistant masters, with hardly an exception, have no idea what hard work means' he wrote to the governors, 'It will undoubtedly take some time to infuse a spirit of work throughout the school'.

To cure the boys' lack of briskness (which is what he meant by absence of discipline), Sanderson introduced class-singing and gymnastics. A drill instructor was appointed and the whole school did physical training twice a week. But the staff was another matter. During the next seven years nearly all of them left, including Brereton and the three senior housemasters.

Walker refers to this period as the 'years of conflict'; an assault by the Head against vested interests opposed to his plans to reorganise the school. Sanderson's critics said that he could only work with a staff of yes-men, and in a sense this was true. Sanderson expected his staff to work with him, not under him. To do that they had to see eye to eye with him. If they didn't, they had to go. Conflict there undoubtedly was, and the strain of overcoming opposition left its mark. It explains the centralised form of control that remained until his death.

One effect of the housemasters' departure was to raise the question of how the houses should be run. Until then they had been treated as private boarding houses from which the housemaster, like any landlord, expected to make a profit. As the clerk to the Grocers' Company complained, when dealing with their claims, 'Once again we see the idea that Oundle is a collection of private schools subsidised by the Grocers' Company, and a consequent claim by outgoing housemasters to dispose of the livestock with the premises'.

Sanderson was determined that this system should be changed, and replaced by hostels owned by the school. He proposed that two semi-detached houses should be built on the playing fields, and sent sketches of what he had in mind to the Company's architect. In the meantime he suggested that the old Sidney House should be rented as a hostel. The Oundle Committee was won round (once again with a majority of a single vote) largely by the argument that the two hostels would make a profit of about £1000 a year for the school funds. Thus the first of the Field Houses came into being – the present Laxton and Crosby block, initially Sydney and Laxton. He also got approval to extend the laboratories, and a new Science wing was opened in 1900.

By the turn of the century Sanderson had secured the confidence of the governors and of the new staff that he himself had appointed. But what about the boys? Some of them recall having lived in constant fear of his wrath. Others admit that there were deliberate efforts to provoke that wrath – not only by such stagey devices as the famous mock trial, but by organised coughing and so on. At first he seems to have distrusted them as much as they distrusted him. But the Mock Trial – a viciously satirical play full of Latin tags and classical allusions – turned out to be the climax of their opposition. His action in ignoring it seems to have won them over. 'It did not seem so funny then,' said one of the authors, 'as it did when we had prepared it.' The Headmaster's reaction showed that he had a sense of style, after all, and schoolboys believe in fair play. They knew that his temper was unpredictable, that a molehill could at any moment become a mountain. But the attitude of the school towards him began to change. And conversely, so did the Head's.

To be sure, the opposition and battles of the first few years caused him to lose his temper frequently. He began as a severe punisher, seizing his victims and thrashing them 'in a hail of swishing strokes that seemed to envelop them'. But later on he came round to the idea of abandoning punishment altogether. In his last ten years there was no beating at all. He would in theory, wrote Walker, have approved of the man who, when asked to write a book on the punishment of crime, found that he wrote instead on the crime of punishment. (It is said that in an examination paper for a university teaching diploma he once set the question: 'Never punish except in anger – discuss'. The proof reader cut out the 'except' – and Sanderson cut out the question.)

Under his new regime the school numbers gradually recovered, though it took him eleven years to reach the best figures of Reade's time. After that the pressure was to keep them in check. Sanderson's natural desire was for the school to grow, not just for the obvious reasons of finance and prestige, but to demonstrate his belief that each boy should be helped to bring out the best that was in him. In a small school there might be two or three boys who would respond to a course in, say, metallurgy or agriculture. But in a larger school there would be enough of them to justify providing proper tuition and equipment for such a course. To widen the curriculum and make it more flexible it was vital that the school should be bigger. 'Numbers,' he told the Oundle Committee, 'were needed in order to organise efficient teaching in the branches of knowledge which ought to be introduced into the school curriculum: there was a field here for useful experimental work.'

Yet in spite of the steady rise in admissions, and indeed a three years' waiting list, the governors remained cautious. In December 1903 the Court told Sanderson that numbers must not be allowed to exceed 250, including day-boys. This blow to Sanderson's hopes was softened, however, by the decision to build another new hostel, for which the name of Cromwell House was suggested, but changed to Grafton – after a celebrated Grocer and printer. The plans for this additional field house envisaged a subsequent extension; indeed the present Sidney appeared alongside Grafton on 1907. At the same time a new house was created to move in beside Laxton. Once again there was talk of calling this Cromwell (though Sanderson favoured Mildmay), but in the end it was named Crosby after Sir John Crosby, the Grocer and diplomat who built Crosby Hall in London. Thus the field houses settled down in the same order as they are today.

And gradually Sanderson infused the governors with his own enthusiasm to expand. By February 1906 the Oundle Committee had gained enough confidence to consider plans for

The Great Hall (above) *was built in 1907-8. The wings were added in 1910.*

further accommodation which would enable the school to be increased to 300. Since the tuition fee had been raised to £25 a year, this made good financial sense. New buildings would add to the school's growing prestige – already, it was noted, parents were choosing between Oundle and schools like Rugby or Malvern – and this in turn might lead to higher fees still. The Committee was therefore receptive to Sanderson's recommendation that a Big Schoolroom should be built on the site of the Red Lion Inn to the north of School House.

Arthur Blomfield, the Company's surveyor, produced plans for an assembly hall with classrooms below, on the lines of the Pears Memorial Hall which his father had designed at Repton. His plans included an extension linking School House to the assembly hall, for the use of the headmaster, and a chapel to the north. But difficulties arose, for no dwelling house could be permitted to overlook the rectory garden. It was therefore decided to build the Great Hall alone, and this was completed in 1908. Two years later, the wings for classrooms were added, though at a reduced height from that envisaged in the original design.

By then Sanderson was pleading for bigger and better laboratories. The Engineering lab, though still unique in a public school, represented the heart of his system for teaching mechanical science. But it needed to be twice the size, and accompanied by a proper Biological laboratory and museum. He produced plans to reconstruct the old building. However, at this point the Court went further than even he had suggested, and approved designs for a completely new science block on land that was being used as allotments on the other side of Milton Road. Constructed of the same honey-coloured Northamptonshire stone as the Great Hall, it contained four large lecture rooms, with a standardising laboratory and teaching museum, a drawing office, a spacious machinery hall, chemistry and biology laboratories. It was finished in August 1914, just as war broke out, and represented a huge advance on the facilities of any other public school in the country.

Like other schools, Oundle had an OTC or Rifle Corps, which had been started in 1902, with W.G. Grace JR, the son of the great Dr Grace, as commanding officer. In parenthesis it should be mentioned that Grace the Younger, a Sanderson appointee who died suddenly in 1905, often brought his father to play cricket at Oundle. In 1897 Dr Grace helped the Masters to beat the School, scoring 54 in the first innings and 4 in the second, and taking nine wickets for 89 runs. Playing for his son's XI in 1901 and 1902, he made 141 and 69. Thus his average for the four innings was 67, and in each case he was dismissed by a catch (which may have a certain significance).

In the early stages of the war many of the older boys rushed to join up, but their places were filled by an influx of younger ones, who stayed longer than expected once the age limit

W.G. Grace, the great cricketer (below right), *played against Oundle when his son was a master. He is standing in front of the old pavilion* (left).

for entering the armed forces was raised. Consequently the number of impending vacancies was reduced, and numbers rose. In 1916 there were 385 boys at Oundle. Sanderson told the Court: 'I must not be blamed for this invasion of the school. It is the call of the time, not necessarily of the time of war, although the war will accentuate the need. A great school of this kind is an urgent need. I think it is what the Court had in mind: Modern – making use of the huge developments of the last fifty years – Classical, humanistic, revealing the true spirit of things . . . The school is what people are asking for, wondering about; and our duty is to show it can be done.'

During the war years the value of his practical training was proved beyond doubt. Indeed Oundle surged ahead so fast that extra accommodation had to be acquired to relieve the pressure, for there simply was not enough room for everyone. And so first Laundimer (Lord Lyvedon's former town mansion) and then Bramston (built about 1700 by Stephen Bramston, the lawyer) were taken over and adapted into houses, just as the Berrystead had been bought and turned into a preparatory house by the Rev. M.W. Brown a few years earlier. These mansions, with the best gardens in Oundle, added to the School's amenities. Even so an overflow of boys had to lodge with married masters, and additional classrooms were rented in unexpected corners. The school was beginning to spread all over the town.

But the most striking feature of all was the work done for the Munitions Board. At first boys from the Engineering side put in eight or nine hours a week producing parts for contractors and the Board itself. Subsequently, a scheme was devised whereby the whole school joined in. Forms went into the workshops in turn for a week of fifty-four hours, and volunteers kept the work going during the holidays. They made tools such as draw-punches,

clamp screws and punch holders; finished off brass parts for torpedoes; fashioned horse-shoes, and produced screens and bed rests for a military hospital. During the course of the war the workshops delivered 12,376 parts to a Peterborough munitions firm, 32,008 tools to Woolwich arsenal, and among other items, produced 1393 large horse-shoes. Yet the normal school work did not suffer. On the contrary, time spent in the workshops seemed to relieve tension among the senior boys and develop what Sanderson described as 'alertness, attention, creativeness'. In fact the wartime experiment proved such a success that 'Shops-week' became a special feature of Oundle which has continued ever since as an integral part of the school curriculum.

Food production was not neglected either. All available pieces of ground, including the Field Houses' lawns, were planted with potatoes or other vegetables, and experimental plots to grow grain were set up on the rugger field now known as the Two Acre. This encouraged Sanderson to press on with a scheme to teach Agriculture as a branch of applied science by starting an experimental farm. And so the 'Dung Sixth' came into being.

Whether its members were so involved in their work that they went on planting, as we are told they did, when an Old Boy crashed his plane against the Workhouse chapel is open to question; certainly everyone rushed to greet another OO who landed on the cricket field. Aeroplanes were still a novelty and the R.F.C. was, of course, still part of the army. All the same an aero engine was sent to the school. and set up in a shed by the armoury for the edification of aspiring pilots.

Throughout the war OTC training went steadily on. Each Friday every boy who was old enough spent the whole day in uniform drilling with the corps and being taught to use

221 Old Boys lost their lives in the First World War. The School workshops produced munitions (the Cloisters are seen left) and the OTC (seen opposite in 1911) continued to train.

fire-arms. What the German prisoners of war who found themselves in Oundle must have thought of these activities on the parade ground and in the workshops must be open to conjecture. They might have been surprised to learn that a wounded officer sent to assist the Corps turned out to be an operatic singer, and promptly put on *The Pirates of Penzance*.

For all this the School always managed to be among the top scorers in the Oxford and Cambridge examinations. Oundle headed the list of Higher Certificates in 1912, 1914, and 1917, and came second to Rugby in 1910 and 1913. Indeed from 1910 to 1917 over six hundred Higher Certificates (corresponding to today's 'A' levels) were won, an average of 35 a year. After 1917 the regulations changed and the examinations were graded into different categories. But in Sanderson's last years, from 1918-22, the success story continued and some 70 Higher, 50 School, and 50 Lower Certificates were secured. It is true that in 1918, when the School was again second to Rugby, the examiners commented unfavourably on some of the writing and spelling. This Sanderson attributed to his policy of making whole forms take the examinations indiscriminately. 'Besides,' he added in a comment that many authors will endorse, 'worrying boys over writing and spelling spoils their creative faculties'.

But the growing casualty lists were depressing: boys could be in school one term and have their names on the Roll of Honour the next. Sanderson's own son was killed in the war, and so were several of the masters. In all 221 Old Boys lost their lives in the First World War; OOs won 3 VCs, 29 DSOs and 3 Bars; 115 MCs and 6 Bars; 4 DFCs, 2 AFCs, 3 DSCs, an MM and a DSM.

When the news of the armistice came on 11 November 1918, there were no celebrations at the headmaster's request. But the following April the school put on a special production of Bernard Shaw's *Arms and the Man*, with Act One adapted for the occasion by the playwright himself, who appeared on stage to accept a 'call' for the first time since the play had been launched twenty-five years before. Arnold Bennett and H.G. Wells were also present as parents; in fact the part of Bluntschli was played by G.P. Wells, the novelist's son.

The decision to raise a fund for a war memorial had already been made, and Sanderson hoped that it would take the form of the chapel he had always wanted. The subscription raised some £15,000, to which the Grocers added £10,000 and the site. Sadly Sanderson did not live to see the Chapel completed and surrounded by its spacious lawns. Nor could he have known that Blomfield's magnificent structure, designed at his request to be in keeping with the style of the Great Hall and the Science block, would be a memorial not only for the Oundelians who had fallen but for Sanderson himself.

In the space of thirty years he had transformed a small ancient school, deadened by more than four centuries of classical fare, into one of the most dynamic and progressive educational establishments in the country. He achieved this by trial and error, by constant experimentation, by finding new ways of doing things, and then putting them into practice.

'When I became headmaster,' he said on the night he died, in the final speech in London to the Union of Scientific Works, which was a sort of personal testament, 'I began by introducing engineering to the school – applied science. The first effect was that a large number of boys who could not do other things could do that. They began to like their work in school. They began to like school. That led on to introducing a large number of other sciences, such as agricultural chemistry, horse-shoeing (if that is a science), metallurgical chemistry, bio-chemistry, agriculture.

'Then I ventured to do something daring. We began to replace explicit teaching by finding out. We did this first with these newly introduced sciences. Then we began to impress the aims and outlook of science on to other departments of school life. History, for instance: we began to replace the old class-room teaching and learning by a laboratory for history, full of books and other things required in abundance, so that boys in all parts of the school could find out the things we required for today. We set them to find out things for the service of science, the service of literature, modern languages, music.

'This began to change the whole organisation of the school, its aims and methods. It was no use organising boys into forms by the ordinary methods of promotion for this sort of work. You have to make up your mind what you have to do, and then go about and collect anybody who would be of service to that particular work. You would require boys of one characteristic and boys of another. You make them up into teams for the particular work they have to do. The boys who do not fit into this or that particular work must have some other particular work found for them. And so you begin to design the work of the school for them.

'Now, presently you discover, when you do this, that not a single boy exists who is not wanted for some particular work. Each has his place in the team, and in his place he is as important as any other boy. Placing them in order of merit does not work any more. The scientific method absolutely changed the position towards class lists and order of merit.'

Sanderson went on to argue that the love of work for its own sake spreads; ultimately everyone is affected and relishes the service he is rendering to the community. Finally, competition dwindles and passes away, so that you have reached what appears to be a change in human nature.

H.G. Wells, who was in the chair, recalls that Sanderson then paused and smiled in a breathless manner, half panting, half laughing. His glasses gleamed at the audience as he delivered his final message.

'We must send out workers imbued with the determination to seek and investigate truth – and to take great care that in that search for truth they will never take part in or sympathise with those methods by which the edge of truth is blunted.'

The voice stopped. Someone pushed up a chair and Sanderson sat down. And then, with the applause still ringing in his ears, he slumped to the ground. Wells could not believe it when he learned that he was dead.

To sum up, then, it can be said that if Busby was the first of the great revitalizing headmasters, raising Westminster in the seventeenth century to a pitch it was not to reach

Sanderson sought to replace 'explicit teaching' by 'finding out' particularly in the newly introduced sciences. Above Alan Rayden demonstates a chemistry experiment.

again until today, Sanderson was in a sense the last. He was a radical reformer; yet like Arnold and Thring he worked within the framework of the public school system. Single-handed, he remoulded an ancient but relatively obscure school, which only twenty years previously had progressed from grammar to public school status, and turned it into a flourishing establishment that was ahead of the others in employing the more advanced ideas of the age. He achieved this against considerable opposition, by fighting the old allegiances, by replacing the ingrained ideologies of the public school system with his own progressive concepts.

Moreover he was not merely a believer in the educative value of science and engineering. Sanderson also had an ethical ideal. He maintained that individual creativeness should go hand in hand with a spirit of cooperation. While wanting boys to concentrate on the things they did best, be believed that they should collaborate together rather than work individually, and thus bring into being this spirit of cooperation. What he disliked most in other schools was the competitive atmosphere. Rather than compete against each other, he felt that boys should be spurred by the feeling that their personal exertions were contributing to the communal effort.

Sometimes one suspects, indeed, that had it been possible, Sanderson would have wished to see modern industry revert to a collection of medieval guilds, with masters and apprentices, just as it was in Florence until quite recent times. As his biographer observed, 'Sanderson aimed at nothing less than the creation of a new order of knights-errant, who should save society by reorganizing it'. (To which Mack comments that his knights-errant, tilting at the windmill of industrialism, sound uncomfortably like A.H. Clough making a Sunday school out of Oxford.)

Of course the twentieth century was hardly to prove the right setting for creative spirits who preferred to cooperate rather than compete. Yet this was very much part of the liberal ethos (derived to some extent from Arnold, but above all from Ruskin) which always tended to emphasise moral rather than intellectual attitudes. Indeed, it was a natural reaction to Victorian materialism. Moreover, if Sanderson was inclined to lay rather too much stress on ethical ideas, in other ways he went further than most liberals were prepared to do. For instance, he encouraged militarism and the OTC, and welcomed the war – though eventually it brought disillusion and made him revise 'his shattered conceptions of the state and duty'.

Though not in Orders, he was a religious man, and his sermons played a large part in what Wells called 'Sanderson contra Mundum' – the schoolmaster who set out to conquer the world. He was a confused, abundant speaker, whose ideas poured out in a torrent of jerks and digressions. In a single address he would jump from the story of the rich man to a commentary on Marx and Lenin; then to the proposed memorial chapel and the proper use of artistic ability; and after articulating on the difference between creative wealth and consumptive wealth, he would end up discoursing on the possible exhaustion of the coal supply and the necessity of using other sources of energy. Yet the boys loved these oratorial flights, and those who parodied the 'Old Man's' quaint but rich turns of speech were often the ones who appreciated them most.

'I learned a great deal from him,' said Dr. Needham, the noted scientist, when he opened the new Physics Block on 24 September 1988. 'One of the things I remember best was his emphasis on "spaciousness". "You should think spaciously, me boy", he used to say; and I am sure I would never have started the "Science and Civilization in China" project, which will run to at least 27 volumes, if I had not had that adjuration ringing in my ears. In another way I was greatly helped by my workshop experience, then obligatory, even for the Classical Sixth. For when I came to the mechanical engineering volume I had, as part of my natural background, a practical acquaintance with lathes and milling machines. I seem to remember also that on one occasion Sanderson cancelled all the inter-house matches because he said that cooperation rather than competition was the order of the day. Afterwards he rescinded the order – but the message had got through to where it belonged'.

H.G. Wells, the most widely read and influential British writer of his time, published a biography of his friend Frederick Sanderson in 1924:

'Of all the men I have ever met, only one has stirred me to a biographical effort,' he wrote,

Above: *a recent project in the metal workshops nears completion.*

'I think him beyond question the greatest man I have ever known with any degree of intimacy. To tell his story is to reflect on all the main educational ideas of the last half century, and to revise our conception of the process and purpose of the modern community in relation to education . . . By all ordinary standards the Oundle School of his later years was a brilliant success; I saw my own sons get an education there better than I had ever dared hope for in England.'

X

LIFE'S RICH PAGEANT

OUNDLE UNDER DR FISHER

T O FOLLOW SUCH A MAN was no easy task. Sanderson was an innovator. But the need now was for a consolidator rather than another educational reformer. This role Dr Fisher carried out with conspicuous success. Although he inherited problems such as excessive numbers, improvised buildings, and tangled finances, he managed in a business-like and persuasive fashion to carry the governing body with him and overcome most of the difficulties, so that at the end of his twenty-three years as Head, Oundle's prestige as a forward-looking school was not only maintained but enhanced.

Chosen from a list of fifty-six candiates, Kenneth Fisher was the son of a Lancashire cotton merchant. He was born in 1882 and went from Manchester Grammar School to Magdalen College, Oxford. After a spell at Jena University, where he received a PhD for chemistry, he carried on his work in the laboratories of Manchester University, and accompanied a scientific expedition to investigate rubber production – even going to the source of the Niger, which had been discovered by Mungo Park's kinsman. Subsequently he became head of the Chemistry department at Clifton College. For most of the war years he managed the Ministry of Munitions plant at Winnington, Northwich, which was producing a new form of high explosive. He was senior Science master at Eton at the time of his appointment at Oundle.

As a scientist, Dr Fisher experienced none of the difficulties that marred Sanderson's early years. No doubt this was due to a sense of loyalty to the school's new identity which was now shared by both masters and boys. But his own gifts of kindliness and humour certainly helped. Unlike Sanderson, who tended to conduct much of his business in the roadway between School House and the Cloisters, he preferred the privacy of his own study. Even so, he was instantly available to anyone who wished to see him, though he could display a masterly inactivity if he thought the problem did not concern him. He was a keen ornithologist and a competent golfer; from his portly figure and rubicund face – not for nothing was he nicknamed 'Bud' – you would not have guessed that he played wing three-quarter for his county at rugger.

That his task was one of maintenance, Dr Fisher never doubted. After gaining ground so quickly, the school had to make good its position. The saying 'Sanderson built in a hurry and Fisher put in the drains' was often literally true, for it was necessary to install new drains and rewire most of the converted houses into which the school had sprawled, octopus-like, all over the town. Even so, there was still a lack of space.

One of Dr Fisher's first actions was to move the school bookshop into the elegant pillared building facing the market-place (where it has remained, to become known in publishing circles as one of the best-stocked bookshops in the Midlands).Next, the British school in Milton Road, which Sanderson had intended to use as Music rooms, was turned into a club house for the domestic staff, and the Music schools were installed in a house called 'The Firs' to the north of the Home Close, with eleven rooms to contain pianos, orchestral equipment, the music library and record collection.To meet the difficulty of finding accommodation for married masters in a town the size of Oundle, Fisher continued the policy of acquiring suitable quarters as they came on the market, and in the course of time all but a very few members of the staff were lodged in property owned by the governing body.

A financial reconstruction was already under way when the new Head took over, for with the growth of the school the old system of accountancy could no longer bear the strain. Fisher inherited a financial secretary with a clerical staff. But for the first time he appointed a Bursar to be responsible for procuring supplies and keeping the school property in order. Before long it became evident that in an expanding institution like Oundle, the Bursar was a key figure second only in importance to the headmaster himself.

Numbers were the perennial problem. When Sanderson died, there were 532 boys in the school, and in his first term Fisher had to find room for 541. The governors' policy was to keep this figure down to five hundred, and they asked him to comply. It was realised, however, that a reduction immediately after the arrival of Sanderson's successor might damage the school's reputation. The upward pressure was therefore tacitly allowed to continue, and by the following year it proved impossible to keep numbers below the 550 mark. By 1925, 523 boys were crammed into houses intended to accommodate 480 at the most, and some 40 others were either farmed out with married masters or put up in what were known as 'holding' houses.

Once it became obvious that the numbers would not fall in the foreseeable future and that to plan in terms of five hundred was out of the question, the Oundle committee began to consider providing accommodation for at least ninety extra boys in a new double block to be run as hostels by single masters. For his part, Dr Fisher argued in favour of a separate house with a married man in charge. In the end it was necessary to have both. St Anthony House was built in 1926, on the site known as Shillibeer's. But ten years later, when the governors saw that the existing houses were still over-crowded and Dryden's old building was no longer adequate, a new double block with married quarters was erected at the northern end of the Home Close. Here Dryden moved in January 1938, and a new house named Sanderson came into being that April under the charge of Mr W.G. Walker. As things turned out, it was providential. Only three months earlier Sydney House had been badly damaged by fire, and its inmates were able to put up in old Dryden while their own house was being rehabilitated.

Meanwhile there was a byzantine maze of forms to be faced. The functions of the Classical and History Sixths were clear. But who could guess that ScVIA1α1 taught Pure Science, whereas ScVIA1α2 was for biologists; that ScVIA1β1 did applied science, ScVIβ2 took agriculture, but ScVIA2β was concerned with modern languages?

Having tidied up the nomenclature – for instance, the Modern and History Modern Sixths were brought into being – Dr Fisher refined the curriculum; on the principle that the school must be made to suit the boy and not vice versa he added a number of small sets and 'private routines' with the aim that every boy should ultimately get into the Sixth form that suited him. He also displayed a fondness (to some it appeared almost a mania) for examinations. Fourth forms took the Lower Certificate, which though virtually useless, was felt to provide a good training; the Fifth and Removes sat for School Certificates; the Sixth for Higher Certificates. What was normally a two year cycle was covered in half the usual time, and boys who gained a School Certificate (the 'O' levels of today) would attempt the Higher Certificate the following year. As a result the Oundle candidates were younger than those in other schools, and often acquired a profusion of certificates. In 1936, for instance, the figures were 119 Higher, 86 School, and 50 Lower; in Fisher's last year (when the Lower Certificate had been abolished) no less than 122 Higher and 197 School Certificates were secured. Unapproached as they were by any other school, these results led to a feeling, not unmixed with envy, that Oundle's work schedule was geared to pocketing awards.

Maybe so. Yet while other schools declined in the aftermath of the Depression Oundle was bursting, and its successes were not merely academic. Oundle's musical renown was enhanced by performances of great oratorios, such as Handel's *Messiah*, Bach's *Mass in B Minor*, or Mendelssohn's *Elijah*, in which the whole school took part, and which were regularly broadcast by the BBC.

Now, too, Oundle was making a reputation for itself in the sporting world. The school had always played Rugby football, but coached by the legendary Frank Spragg, its first great XV was that of 1929, which contained two future Cambridge blues. This team won all its matches, and between 1935 and 1938 the First XV maintained its supremacy against Bedford, Uppingham, Haileybury, Stowe and Rugby, losing only to Bedford in 1935 and Stowe in 1938. Few who watched the adroit hooking of the scrum, the brisk passing of the halves, the sparkling interplay between the three-quarters, always so precisely in line and never kicking for touch if it could be helped, and the secure hands of the backs, can have doubted that here was school rugger at its best.

Frank Spragg, who won a Cambridge blue for both Rugby football and fives, was brought by Dr Fisher straight from the university, and his coaching at both cricket and fives was hardly less successful. Though Oundle rarely beat Uppingham at cricket, it never lost to either Stowe or the Leys in the Thirties, and apart from drawn matches, had five wins to one defeat against Bedford (in 1940 Bedford won by one run!). At fives, Spragg's influence on the standard of play, and the new covered courts that were built in 1930 (and were

From the early Thirties Oundle – seen in a match against Bedford opposite – excelled at Rugby football, cricket and fives, notably under the guidance of Frank Spragg (right)

sometimes used for the Varsity match) led to a long list of victories in the Public Schools' Championship. During the Thirties the School fives team had an unbeaten record against Rugby, Felsted, St Paul's and Malvern, and only lost once to Bedford (in 1934).

As for other sports, such as rowing, athletics, gymnastics, boxing and swimming, the list of 17 Oxford and 47 Cambridge blues won during Dr Fisher's time speaks for itself. Let it also be said that my friend Michael Mills has achieved an honoured place in the *Guinness Book of Records* along with his son Peter, as the only father and son to have both captained the Cambridge Cricket Eleven in their time.

Looking back, it becomes apparent that some of Kenneth Fisher's appointments showed considerable flair. Apart from Frank Spragg, who was housemaster of St Anthony for so long, he took on C.J. Pennethorne Hughes, the historian and film critic, who later became Controller of Programmes at the BBC, and C.A.B. Marshall, whose bossy headmistress sketches came joyfully over the air in the evening and flowed (at least in gesture and humour) into the classroom a few hours later, to his form's great delight, for he was an inspired teacher and congenial housemaster of New House. 'Cabby' Marshall, like Hughes an OO, was a well-known broadcaster even in those days, and one might have guessed that he would later become, as Arthur Marshall, one of Britain's favourite authors and TV performers.

112

Of Fisher's other appointees, five left to become headmasters in England and abroad, while 'Tub' Shaw, 'Bobby' Burns, Dudley Heesom, Hugo Caudwell (poet, painter, and author of philosophical books), A.C. Cutcliffe, Ian Hepburn, Graham 'Thnappy' Priestman, A.E. Collier, Edward de Ville, R.E. Cordukes and R.E. Fenwick joined Sanderson's greybeards to form a gifted and dedicated team that raised the standard of tuition to a new level over the next three decades.

In the meantime the great new War Memorial Chapel, splendidly surrounded by lawns, was consecrated by the Bishop of Peterborough on 22 November 1923, though the two organs only came into use four years later. The old makeshift chapel, known affectionately as the 'tin tabernacle' then became an art room. In 1934 the new gymnasium was finished, and the previous wooden gym at the north end of the Cloisters made way for an additional block of classrooms. In 1935 a new 'tuckshop', with accommodation for visiting teams, was opened in Milton Road, to be followed the next year by an open-air swimming pool.

Along with the new houses, these were tangible evidence of Fisher's reign. But at the beginning of the Thirties a significant event occurred which passed largely unnoticed, though anyone perusing the school prospectus would have spotted, no doubt with surprise, the statement that Oundle School was 'incorporated by Royal Charter in 1930'.

This was not a printer's error, as Dr Fisher explained to the OO dinner at Grocers' Hall the following February. The Laxtonian reports him as saying:

In the History of the School the year 1930 would always stand out as one of no ordinary importance, for on August 21st the King signed the Royal Charter. This was a matter for congratulation, setting, as it were, the Royal Seal on the status of the School, and removing certain anomalies in its position which carried with them possible sources of danger in the years to come. Now, with the Charter granted, the School has a permanent independent foundation, and we can look forward to the future with assurance all the greater, and at the same time feel as certain as ever that the bond existing between the School and the Grocers' Company could never be weakened.

In short, it set to rights the controversy that had existed ever since Reade made Oundle a public school as distinct from Laxton's Free Grammar School. Henceforth Oundle had being as an entity of its own by virtue of a Royal Charter, and Laxton School remained the beneficiary of Sir William's endowment – to the extent of £41.4.0 a year.

It should not be disguised that essentially this was a financial operation designed to avert any tax liability on the profits which had been ploughed back into the school (as indeed had happened in the case of Brighton College). For the fact was that between the time of the purchases made from Dr Stansbury in 1875 and the granting of the Charter, well over a quarter of a million pounds had been spent in capital outlay on the school, and nearly half this amount came into the Oundle Building Fund from profits earned by the hostels and from tuition fees. To avoid tax liability as a private enterprise belonging to the Grocers' Company, it was necessary to show that these profits were inalienably the profits of the school. So by the Charter the Court of the Grocers' Company was constituted the governing body of Oundle School, and to this body all the property of the school was transferred. In fact, the Grocers transferred it to themselves. The change was semantic: instead of the Master and Wardens being governors of the school, there was a 'Governing Body' comprising the members of the Court. That was all. Nevertheless the link with Sir William Laxton had been broken. Oundle was no longer an endowed school.

On everyday life, this change in status made not the slightest impression: in fact it was not even mentioned in *The Laxtonian* until six months later, and then only in a routine report of an Old Boys' dinner. The life of the school went on as if nothing had happened, as if there had been no break with the past although technically at least, Oundle was now a new foundation.

At this point we might take a quick look at everday life as it was for the average small boy under Dr Fisher.

As in other public schools, Victorian ethics still prevailed, and Fry's legacy lingered on in the shape of strict regulations governing conduct: roll-calls were taken at least twice a day; there were bounds beyond which none but prefects might go; no fraternising was

114

allowed between boys of different houses. The uniform dress was grey flannel suits with waistcoats, stiff collars (Eton collars for new boys) and black ties, or black coats with striped trousers on Sundays. Crested black caps were worn in the winter, straw 'bashers' in the summer term. The tone was oppressively evangelical: prayers before breakfast, prayers in the Great Hall before school, prayers in the evening; at least two chapel services on Sundays, plus holy communion for those who had been confirmed; scripture lessons after chapel; the usual complement of house prayers. Grace before every meal. And so on, and so on.

Daily life was regulated by bells – Betjeman's 'inexorable bells, to early school, to chapel, to school again: compulsory constipation, hurried meals . . . ' The pressure to hurry everywhere, from classroom to classroom with armfuls of books; to change hastily and rush up to the field for games or OTC drill; to plunge in one's turn into hip baths full of hot muddy water left by the previous occupant, or cold hip baths for a mandatory twenty seconds before breakfast or early school; to hand one's exeat card to the housemaster within the required space of time when one had been to some extra-mural activity – the dread of being late was perpetually present. But all this was stoically accepted as an inherent part of school life. There was very little time for leisure in Fisher's Oundle, which meant that there was not much scope for mischief either. This was, of course, the underlying motive for keeping every moment of the day filled with some planned activity, so that a sort of amnesia was necessary to keep up with the stringent and single-minded routine. Covert longings there may have been, *affaires de coeur* undoubtedly occurred, but sensual lusts were effectively thwarted. There was, I would say, very little if any of the sexual horseplay which apparently disfigured school life elsewhere, and which Oundle boys simply regarded as 'smut'.

Here I cannot resist quoting a passage from Arthur Marshall's delightful autobiography, *Life's Rich Pageant*:

There were a number of rules which [it was] evidently hoped were a foolproof recipe for chastity. A boy could not speak to anyone a year older than himself. Smiles too were out, for smiling (and few human activities are pleasanter) spelt danger, a go-ahead to depravity. Conversely a boy could not speak to or smile at anybody younger than himself. A boy could in no circumstances mix socially with a boy of whatever age in another house. This was for some muddled reason thought to be especially perilous.

Every so often Mr Hale, a gifted speaker, delivered himself of a moral lecture designed to scare the pants off one and all . . . He had composed a striking opening sentence: 'This house is a midden'. Only the cleverer boys knew what a midden was (I was fourteen and unclued-up on middens) but the word's general meaning became clear as the pijaw progressed. . . When all was over and we were dismissed, gifted mimics got busy on the speech and as we disrobed for bed, key phrases rang round the dormitories: 'This house is a midden': 'This thing wrecks lives': 'It is not the top of the house': in all, a robust reaction.

At this period Oundle cultivated the image of a tough, no-nonsense school. Lacking perhaps the polish, the airs and graces, of some of the great foundations in the South, it displayed the down-to-earth qualities of the Midlands or the North country, from which a great proportion of its alumni came. Because of its engineering tradition, Oundle tended to attract the sons of parents with family businesses or industrialists; indeed the school lists bristled with household names, from jam to toothbrushes, dreadnaughts to cars. (At Crosby, for instance, the son of Lord Austin's chief executive sat opposite the son of the managing director of Morris Motors: their fathers, in fierce competition, produced half of Britain's transport. John Lyons of Jaguar's turned up a little later.)

This emphasis on science and engineering was reflected in two unique features: Shops Weeks, and Conversazione. Every form, from the lowest to the highest, stopped normal work and spent a week of each term in the workshops – either the metal shops or the foundry, the woodshops or the forge – learning to work lathes and chisels, bellows and anvils. It was a welcome break from the classroom, though classical students were usually quite pleased to return to their books after a 54 hour stint at manual labour.

On the other hand Conversazione, held every Speech Day, was a display of group projects, carried out partly during school hours and partly in the boys' own time, which had to do with such things as building engines, working out experiments in geology or chemistry, setting up biology tests and so on. They called for a good deal of ingenuity from both masters and boys, for the participants had not only to devise the exhibits and make them work, but explain them to parents who were often professional researchers and manufacturers. For example, one exhibit comprised a series of experiments reconstructed as Faraday had performed them.

Sometimes indeed they were highly sophisticated. In 1937, when television was still at an exploratory stage, a set was rigged with the help of Baird (whose son was at the school) and the BBC, enabling viewers to watch a programme transmitted from London. This was a dozen years before the BBC opened its earliest TV service, which even then only reached the London area.

Moreover the experiments and demonstrations were not limited to scientific subjects. Maps, charts, and models of the work done in history and geography were on show, among them artefacts from excavations at Fotheringhay and Thorpe Waterville. One exhibit traced the development of transport by land and sea; another was a draft Peace Treaty drawn up by the History Sixth. There were also models of ancient theatres and a series of plays including a French ballet and scenes from *The Beggar's Opera*. All this went to prove the truth of John Newton's dictum, which was printed on the cover of the programme: 'I cannot tell whether anything be better learned than that which is learned by play.'

If World War II caught the school, like the nation, unprepared (with all the black-out to do), Oundle rapidly returned to the pattern of the previous conflict. The workshops received orders and set about filling them; boys went out to help the farmers with their beet, potatoes and threshing. Yet there were differences. For one thing, food and clothing were

Above *As war looms (1938), masters try on gas masks.*
From the left they are: Squire, Fenwicke, Collier, Malan, Kingham, Burns, Hepburn, Caudwell,

immediately rationed. Housemasters no longer changed for dinner, as they had always done, dinner jackets being hardly the most suitable attire for fire-watching; the boys got steadily shabbier. The town was filled with evacuees. There was no room to put parents up – had they petrol to come – or had there been any Speech Days to visit.

More important, since the system of calling-up made it unnecessary to rush and enlist, boys waited to be conscripted. Numbers in the school therefore went on increasing, from 581 in 1941 to 652 in 1945, and somehow they were squeezed in without extra property having to be acquired.

Here Oundle was luckier than some other schools whose premises were commandeered. Malvern, for instance, had its buildings summarily requisitioned twice by the Ministry of

Dr Fisher (right), *headmaster from 1922-45, consolidated the achievements of the Sanderson era.*

Works, and might have had to close down completely – as Wycombe Abbey girls' school was forced to do – but for the generous act of the Duke of Marlborough, who allowed them to use Blenheim Palace in 1940, and subsequently Harrow, who took Malvern in when its site was suddenly needed for the Radar Establishment. And there were other similar dislocations, for instance the City of London School had to move to Marlborough.

At Oundle, boys were trained in fire-fighting, first aid, and dealing with incendiaries. Plans for dispersal were drawn up, and a Report Centre with its observer post on the school playing field was manned night and day by a rotation of masters and boys. Fortunately the town was never bombed, despite the presence of RAF aerodromes in the vicinity. Boys and staff, including the headmaster, joined the Home Guard whose Sunday parades meant that khaki-clad figures, hot from training, arrived in the classrooms to continue, as the most natural thing in the world, their instruction in the Gospel or Old Testament prophecy or whatever it was.

Grocers' Hall escaped destruction in the Blitz, though unhappily a flying bomb turned the library into rubble from which the records were dug out more or less intact, and in 1940 the Master of the Company was killed whilst fire-watching.

But even if Oundle was out of the danger zone, the responsibility, and particularly the growing casualty lists began to take their toll on the headmaster. When the war in Europe ended, it became known that he intended to retire at the end of the summer term in 1945. At the first Speech Day to be held for five years, Dr Fisher introduced Mr G.H. Stainforth, a housemaster at Wellington, who had been appointed as his successor.

Then he read the familiar lesson 'This is the end of the matter, all hath been heard. . . ' and retired to the Old Rectory at Achurch, only a few miles away.

Sadly these words were his swan song, for in the first week of the new term, when visiting Oundle, he suddenly collapsed and died. And with him ended another chapter of history.

XI

MUSCULAR CHRISTIANITY

PUBLIC SCHOOL TRADITIONS IN THE EARLY TWENTIETH CENTURY

"They had the Eton something or the Harrow something. I felt I was nearer to grasping what the something is than ever before. It is a sleek happiness that comes of a shininess which only Eton – or Harrow – can impart. The nearest thing to it must be boot polish."

J.M. Barrie, in a letter to Lady Asquith, 1920

BURNISHED AND BLITHE, embued with that tranquil consciousness of effortless superiority which Asquith (City of London School) ascribed to the denizens of Balliol College Oxford the cream of British youth, nurtured on the cricket field, weaned on the *Boys Own Paper*, trained from breakfast to lights out in the ideals of manliness and godliness, spread throughout Victoria's Empire to take up the White Man's Burden (to seek another's profit, and work another's gain. Et cetera . . . et cetera).

Reality or illusion? Sophistry or myth? It is time, perhaps, to take a look at the public schools in their bluffest, most heroic period. It is no coincidence that this romantic heyday, stretching roughly from the first Headmasters' Conference in 1869 to the end of the Second World War, coincided with the apogee of the imperial theme, when maps hanging on classroom walls showed (in lavish chunks of red) that a quarter of the world was subject to the Crown's authority, and when education was firmly designed to stress the superiority of all things British.

Take Eton – aristocratic, worldly, metropolitan. The Education Act of 1868 had forced the school to put its own house in order rather than have it done from outside, causing the headmaster, Dr Balston, to resign in protest. He was succeeded first by Hornby, and subsequently by Edmond Warre. Both of these men were fine athletes who encouraged games and the cliquish attitudes that went with them. Steeped in the literature of Greece and Rome, they were flag-waving imperialists whose romanticism was stirred by martial adventures. Percy Lubbock wrote in *Shades of Eton* that Warre was not so much a schoolmaster as a 'leader, a statesman, a prime minister'. Well, maybe so. He certainly helped to form the atmosphere of the school in late Victorian days, when Eton was distinctly more civilized than it had been before.

By then the horrors of Long Chamber, the wholesale floggings of Keate, had passed into history. Granted, there was still a good deal of bullying, and too much beating. But the tone of the place had changed. Partly this was due to a shift in social attitudes. But principally

it came from the concentration on games, which resolved so many of the problems of segregating several hundred boys for two-thirds of the year. The mere fact of siphoning off their energy on the playing fields reduced the likelihood of boys becoming involved in less desirable activities. Nor had the advantages of sport to health and morality passed unnoticed in that golden age of muscular Christianity.

Having known, as collegers, what Eton had been like before organised games were introduced, both Hornby and Warre supported them enthusiastically, while doing their utmost to cultivate the sense of team spirit. The philistinism (an unfortunate word) that came with it was perhaps less desirable. However, as Richard Ollard remarks, in *An English Education*, the foppery of colours and the 'conversion of Pop', the Eton Society – in whose debates Gladstone had won his spurs – into a pantheon for sportsmen was wholeheartedly approved by the vast majority of boys.

In this aura of philathleticism, life tended to centre on the opportunities it offered to those who were good at games or showed promise on the river. Eton became a great games-playing school whose cricketers could take their place in a first class side, and whose oarsmen carried off trophies at Henley.

Refulgent in their tasselled caps, silk scarves and immaculate whites, these sportsmen were the grandees of every public school. In the historian Mack's view, the years between 1870 and 1890 saw 'the greatest upsurge of passionate adoration' focused on games that had ever been known. And blossoming in the increasingly competitive spirit of the age, this

this veneration (now reserved for pop stars) was spurred on, especially among the new plutocracy, by a jingoist sentimentality. It was only necessary to add a dash of drama to get Sir Henry Newbolt's 'breathless hush in the Close tonight – ten to make and the match to win! Play up! Play up! and play the game!' ('Vitai Lampada')

Yes, that was it: 'Play up! Play up! and play the game!' For Eton, the saving grace was that the classics, brilliantly taught by a succession of outstanding scholars such as Cory, Ainger, Luxmoore and Benson, maintained their supremacy. The tradition of classical scholarship, the training of critical faculties, the insistence on a cultivation of taste in literature and the arts, were what gave Eton its power of resistance to the cult of games and colours that swept over Victorian public schools like an engulfing tide.

Of course sporting activities had always been an important part of English life, and indeed Etonians gained quite a reputation for their cricket in the eighteenth century. At Cambridge they used to challenge the rest of the university and regularly beat them. The matches against Harrow began at the turn of the century, and in the earliest recorded contest, which took place in 1805, Byron scored 7 and 2 for Harrow and then went off and got drunk. But in those days matches were played not for the sake of fitness or team spirit, but solely for

Cricket at Repton, c.1900 (opposite) by J.F. Barraud, exemplifies the cult of games, especially cricket, which swept the Victorian public schools. Cricketers in their immaculate whites were the grandees of every public school. Below A match at Charterhouse.

amusement. They were quite unofficial, and tended to be frowned on by the authorities, who questioned their value. 'Of what importance is it in after life,' asked the *Edinburgh Review* in 1810, ' whether a boy can play well or ill at cricket, or row a boat with the skill and precision of a waterman?' Sidney Smith considered such activities useless and regretted ' the ridiculous stress laid on them by the public schools'. Yet games flourished all the same. Regulations for football were codified before 1822 when William Webb Ellis 'with a fine disregard for the rules' picked up the ball and ran with it in his hands, and rugger was born.

As a matter of fact, it is often thought that Arnold was responsible for introducing the cult of athleticism into Britain's public schools. Like many of the myths that came to surround that forceful and eclectic man, it is quite untrue. Actually, Arnold had no time for games and found the exuberance of boys 'more morally distressing than the shouts and gambols of a set of lunatics'.

What Arnold did introduce to Rugby was the concept of manliness – which soon became another of the great Victorian obsessions. He believed that this was the ideal for a Christian gentleman: that only through moral and religious knowledge could a boy be made manly. The chapel was the centre of his ethics, not the playing field. It was Thomas Hughes who, by blending the two together and serving them up neat in *Tom Brown's Schooldays*, gave the notion of manliness a more rugged look.

Hughes, a 'kind of John Bull regenerate', hit on a successful literary genre which was to be widely imitated. Published a few years after Kingsley's *Westward Ho!* launched the ideal of Muscular Christianity (with the help of Leslie Stephen), Hughes' seminal, if misleading, novel helped to produce a 'Tom Brown' stereotype in the many new establishments seeking public school status. Youngsters took eagerly to the idealised picture of life at Arnold's Rugby, and adopted Tom's love of team games. ' It is from them that the readiness, pluck, and self-dependence of the English gentleman are principally caught. They prevent the intellectual superiority from being the only one formally recognised in our education.'

Once the idea had caught on, how quickly it was put into practice! Clifton, Marlborough and Wellington became strongholds of athleticism; Tonbridge introduced cricket colours in 1858. Even the 'inner seven' went with the tide. Games were 'recognised' at studious Shrewsbury, where football became compulsory. Winchester bought land for pitches; Rugby invested in fives courts, cricket pavilions, a gym and a swimming pool. Eton appointed a games master. True, some headmasters viewed the momentum of professionalised games with misgivings. But they could not resist the new worship without injuring the status of their schools once rivalry increased and the *Public School Magazine* began to publish results.

Oundle did not feature in the early issues of this publication, because Reade had not yet got to work. So to see how the games craze was put to good use, let us travel twelve miles north to Uppingham.

'Games are wondrous vital powers,' Thring once declared, 'and a true school life will deal with them as of the highest educational value.'

He celebrated his appointment as Uppingham's headmaster with a whole holiday and a cricket match, recording in his diary that he got 15 by 'some good swinging hits' to the delight of his few pupils (who themselves recalled that his batting was distinctly 'rustic', and that he bowled fast underarm spins which bounced along the ground or reached the wicket-keeper's hands full toss).

Football, initially played to Thring's own rules during his first winter at the school, was described in the style of a classic epic:

> And then they all snatched at the ball to move it forwards in various ways. (For recently the Master in Charge had taught them how the peoples of old had often had contests with races that were fierce.) In the same way now they all ran together in throngs; then again in flight they made different patterns as they ran, imitating the epic battles of old as they charged.

Like 'two great opposing armies' the whole school used to play at once, with Thring and his masters joining in. 'It was an opportunity devised by Providence,' he thought, 'to enable small boys to work off their original sin.' Boys got rid of their pugnacity, and learnt to give and receive hard knocks with good grace.

Before long a games committee was formed, and athletic sports were introduced, consisting of steeple-chases, high and long jumps, a hundred yards race, and throwing the cricket ball, in all of which Thring himself took part. Later a mile and quarter-mile events were added, along with hurdle races.

Games and athletics were important factors in his scheme of education and when the gymnasium was opened in 1859 – the first at any school, with an instructor from Berlin in charge – the gymnastic competition ranked as an end of term examination along with other subjects. 'Plenty of exercise, mental and bodily, is the secret of a good school', was one of Thring's maxims, and it worked wonders. From 25 boys the numbers swelled to 200 in 1863 and 300 in 1865. By that time Uppingham regarded itself as a fully-fledged public school. All the same, an invitation to stage a cricket match with Rugby was rebuffed, and the Eleven had to be content with a fixture against Rossall up at Fleetwood instead.

Such preoccupation with status may seem trivial, were it not that Thring was continuously fighting for the existence of the school. A running battle with the governors to gain financial support for its rapid expansion, to say nothing of struggles with the Endowed Schools Commission – which led to the first Headmasters' Conference at Uppingham in 1869 – occupied much of his time and energy. But both Thring and his Old Boys wanted Uppingham to take its place alongside the other 'great' schools, and they knew that a good reputation on the playing field was the surest way of getting there. Indeed the OUs clubbed together and paid for H.H. Stevenson to be the resident cricket professional.

Stevenson of Surrey had been in the first English side to visit Australia, where twelve matches were played in 1862, thereby paving the way for future Tests. He was noted for having stumped 'W.G'. for a duck in the opening first-class innings of Grace's legendary career. Stevenson was considered by Dr. Grace to be one of the best coaches of young players in the country, and under his guidance such progress was made that the *Cricket Annual* for 1873 rated the Uppingham XI among the top public schools teams. In 1877 five Uppinghamians played for Cambridge, and the school was already becoming famous as a nursery of great cricketers. Commenting on this significant contribution to the games cult, the school's historian, Bryan Matthews, wrote wryly that 'It was almost as if, in his search for the education of the whole boy, Thring helped to create a monster that got out of control.'

Monster perhaps – but a century ago it was an essential part of the public school ethos. Every one of them was characterised by the same pattern of boarding houses, prefects and fags, and the system whereby corporate life and discipline outside the classroom were left in the hands of the senior boys with a minimum of interference from the masters. It was unfortunate, to be sure, that games should have assumed such an excessive importance in the scheme of things, so that sporting 'bloods' became the lords of creation. Yet their very success on the playing field and the veneration they enjoyed from their juniors helped to keep the machinery running smoothly and prompted a powerful *esprit de corps*.

Each school developed its own traditions, its customs, its slang. At Winchester, it took weeks to learn them all. But even the new foundations quickly invented an esoteric array of taboos, privileges, conventions – and, of course, a school song, whose melody voiced a romantic attachment to the Alma Mater; a filial attachment that sometimes lasted for ever. There was the old school tie, the old boy club, the old boy teams, the old boy masters.

It was a curious enchantment, this umbilical cord that linked so many men to their public schools whether they were happy there or not. For instance, Somerset Maugham, who was miserable at King's, Canterbury, nevertheless arranged for his ashes to be buried at the school. When Stanley Baldwin became Prime Minister, his first thought was to form a cabinet 'of which Harrow would be proud'.

There is a story that when he was coming up to London by train, a fellow passenger lowered his copy of *The Times* and said: 'I beg your pardon, but you're an old Harrovian, are you not?'

Gratified, Mr Baldwin said he was.

'Quite, quite,' said the stranger, 'I was very nearly sure. Yes, you must have left in '86, or was it '87?'

'Five,' Mr Baldwin corrected.

'To be sure. Certainly. You were in Small Houses, if I'm not mistaken. Then you went up to Head's. Am I right? Ah, I thought so. Then you roomed with – with, I mean to say, that lanky chap, Thingummy Minor.'

Mr Baldwin smiled and nodded. The fellow passenger was delighted with himself. 'Absolutely – oh quite. I remember perfectly. And I'll recall your name in just a moment. Don't tell me, it was, I mean is, something like Bailey or Bancroft – no, no, hold on – it has a "win" in it.'

'Baldwin,' the Prime Minister supplied, 'Stanley Baldwin.'

'Of course, of course. It was on the tip of my tongue. Well, well, and tell me, Baldwin, since school, what have you been doing with yourself?'

Yet far from being a joke, the old school tie ranked as one of the most potent influences in contemporary life. And in its heyday that influence was staggering. Like the caste mark on a Hindu's forehead, it was the badge of a ruling class which, without it, would have lost its adjective overnight. The Old School Tie stood not so much for education as for a shared experience, for mutual sufferings and pleasures, for the training to an unquestioned philosophy of life. This (according to the newly founded *Daily Express*) embraced the Ten Commandments, the Lord's Prayer, the Sermon on the Mount, and Kipling's 'If'. As such it provided England, and hence the Empire, with a complete and unofficial, yet all pervading, method of government – which John Bright characterised as 'a gigantic form of outdoor relief for the aristocracy'.

Writing in an early issue of *Esquire* some fifty years ago, Edward Acheson advised his fellow Americans that it was not at all tactless to accuse a man openly of being an Old Haberdasher. On the contrary, he would be delighted that his status as a graduate of the Haberdasher Aske's School at Hampstead had been appreciated. By the same token Old Albanians, Manchurians and Perseans were not ancient foreigners, but sometime students of St Albans, Manchester Grammar, and the Perse School respectively. 'The jargon become more complicated with the Old Carthusians, who were not monks . . . The name Old Salopian has no Freudian content, it is derived from the Norman attempt to pronounce Shrewsbury; Old Stoics aren't Greeks, and graduates of St Bees are, unhappily, called "Old Beghians"'.

No wonder that the public schools were invested with a remarkable mystique, when you consider that Eton and Harrow supplied twelve of the nineteen Prime Ministers between Queen Victoria's accession and World War II, as well as a third of all Cabinet Ministers. The House of Lords and Government buildings all over the world shimmered with the best old school ties; indeed the Empire itself was likened to a vast public school in which the natives were run by prefects while being slowly trained to become prefects so that they could ultimately run the school themselves.

Even fictional characters like Raffles or Bulldog Drummond or Bertie Wooster were overgrown schoolboys with a whiff of Stalky about them. As a matter of fact, much of the glamour was created by the writers of public school stories – a literary genre which was unique in the world and met with extraordinary success.

Tom Brown's Schooldays had started the fashion. Whereupon a succession of Victorian authors (favouring the second rather than the first half of Thomas Hughes' novel) went on to exploit the rich market he had uncovered with priggish offerings such as Dean Farrar's *Eric, or Little by Little* – the kind of book, Hugh Kingsmill thought, that Dr Arnold might have written had he taken to drink. A frowsty formula of chapel and sanatorium was common to most of them. Yet by contriving to make the uneventful routine of school life exciting to their readers, Talbot Baines Reed (*The Fifth Form at St Dominics*), R.S. Warren Bell, Harold Avory, Andrew Home and many others churned out best-sellers with titles such as *The Worst House at Sherborough, Frank's First Term*, and *A Row in the Sixth*. Desmond Coke, a master at Shrewsbury, wrote *The Bending of a Twig* and *The Worm* (which was about a boy who was no good at anything until – as in Tom Brown – he befriended another boy and made good). Some delightfully dotty novels, and even dottier poems, came from the Vicar of Stretton near Oundle under the penname of Cuthbert Bede (he also wrote a history of Fotheringhay). But the ultimate in evangelical nonsense, *Gerald Eversley's Friendship*, was produced by J.E.C. Welldon, who was Churchill's headmaster at Harrow and the man who appointed Sanderson to Dulwich. An excruciatingly wet novel, it was very properly clouted for six by Kipling and Wodehouse.

Kipling, influenced by the first part of *Tom Brown*, immortalised his own schooldays at the United Services College in *Stalky and Co.* And Wodehouse, influenced by Stalky, produced a string of boisterous schoolboy yarns, full of games, ragging and study teas, with occasional academic tags that were not out of place in serials for public school magazines. They were written for boys rather than parents (though grown-ups devoured them too) and neatly capture the spirit of the Edwardian era. Thus the games 'blood' was more glamorous than the Balliol scholar – in fact, the swot was a figure of mild derision. Ragging and rule-breaking were good things; to be adept at these was the next best thing to eminence in games. But even if you played cricket for your county in the holidays, you were not expected to 'put on side', i.e. brag about it. This was the Edwardian code, yet the stories still read well.

In the first forty years of this century the market for such fiction was tremendous. Boys' weeklies – and there were at least twelve of them, headed by the venerable *Boys Own Paper* were full of public school tales. *The Gem* and *The Magnet* contained nothing else; each issue being devoted to a continuous serial about the adventures of Harry Wharton and Co, or Bob Cherry and his friends, with Billy Bunter, the 'fat owl of the Remove' at Greyfriars, and The Hon. Arthur A. D'Arcy at St Jim's. All these stories, were written by the same author, Frank Richards, in real life Frank Hamilton. (His wife 'Hilda Richards' wrote girls' school stories with interchangeable characters: her fat girl was called Bessie, and was Billy Bunter's sister.) Since Frank Richards had not been to a public school himself, the atmosphere he depicted was sheer fantasy; in fact it was a caricature. If anything, this added to the fun. But it gave uninitiated readers an entirely false impression of what went on.

Summing up the craze for public school fiction, C.E. Raven wrote in 1928: 'Take a juvenile athlete as your chief ingredient. Add a wit, a bully, a persecuted fag, an awkward scholar, a faithful friend, a dangerous rival and a batch of distorted pedagogues; mix them up in an atmosphere of genial romanticism; insert a smoking scandal, a fight, a cribbing scene, sundry rags, a house match or two; bring them all to the boiling point when the hero scores the winning try or does the hat-trick; serve the whole hot with a title associating the dish with which the initiated can identify; and the suburbs will raid the libraries for the result.'

Of course there were plenty of dissenting voices, and distinguished authors such as George Orwell, Cyril Connolly, Robert Graves and Graham Greene wrote scathingly about the public schools of that period. But the fact remains that no other kind of school has ever had the benefit of so much propaganda; and thousands of young people who were educated at public expense or at small private schools dreamed wistfully of a glorious if illusory life they could only read about.

There is no need to become too indignant about this; after all, the schoolboy hero was then fulfilling the same role as the pop star of today. What could be criticised in the Public Schools of the time was the emphasis on character rather than brains. A handful of clever boys were crammed to win scholarships. The others often learnt little that was of much use to them. But as a result of strenuous physical exercise, a cultivation of the school spirit and a conservative curriculum, they ended up as sound men of their class. Discipline was stern, inflexible, and sometimes absurd. Yet the system suited average boys who were eager to play games and subsequently enforce an equally oppressive way of life at home or overseas; lads who would in their turn mould public opinion. Though the system was hardly in tune with the needs of the sensitive child with unusual interests, it mirrored the values of parents who had themselves been at public schools. This was a period of firmly consolidated class rule and these schools, as we have said, were the nurseries of the nation's leaders. They fostered an imperialist and evangelical spirit that was fashionable at the time. Boys enthusiastically joined the Rifle Corps or Junior Volunteer Corps (the forerunners of the OTC) when the war in South Africa whipped up patriotic fever (at Haileybury they celebrated the relief of Ladysmith by taking an unauthorised half holiday and marching in a cheering procession through Hertford and Ware. For which the headmaster, Edward Lyttelton, who had pro-Boer sympathies, personally beat 72 senior boys, one of whom was Clement Attlee.)

If democracy and socialism were still bad words in Edwardian days, the political, social and economic problems which confronted George V were immense. Indeed his twenty-five year reign was marked by a continuous series of crises – starting with a constitutional crisis, World War I, the emergence of the Parliamentary Labour Party, the General Strike, the massive economic depression of the early Thirties, the collapse of the hopes for world peace and, towards the end, the rise of the European dictators. And yet, against the background of these cataclysmic events, the public schools sailed serenely on, as if Marx and Freud had never existed. The upper classes still seemed to be isolated and content, and the system of education that had been evolved for them continued to conform to the same old pattern. Children went from prep school to public school and then to the university or Sandhurst or some family concern as a matter of course. Oxford and Cambridge were largely populated by public school men who treated their varsity days as a happy interlude between school and the adult world; many hardly bothered whether they got a degree or not.

'From the first I regarded Oxford as a place to be inhabited and enjoyed for itself and not as a preparation for anything else,' wrote Evelyn Waugh. 'Most of my associates, including many who have been highly successful in later life, went down with bad degrees or with none at all.'

Since the *ancien régime* encouraged this system, the public schools were able to maintain their monolithic structure – their privileges and colours and complex hierarchies – right up until the middle of this century. There were even some newcomers: Rendcombe was founded in 1920, Stowe and Canford in 1923, Bryanston in 1928, Gordonstoun in 1935. Even the grammar schools, some of which had grown considerably in the prewar years, tended to model themselves increasingly on the public school pattern. So, unfortunately, did many of the girls' schools (thereby presenting the world, as Vivian Ogilvie irascibly observes, with the psychological monstrosity of the woman who goes through life trying to perpetuate her own boyhood).

Thanks to Sanderson, Oundle was able to discard some of the traditional constraints that shackled most schools. Nevertheless, he had to work within the limits of the system. Consequently, when Graham Stainforth took over from Dr Fisher in 1945, he found that for all its progressive thrust, Oundle was still very much part of the club.

Right Graham Stainforth, headmaster from 1945-56, placed greater emphasis on the Humanities. Arthur Marshall wrote of him: 'He did great good and deserves the highest marks.'

XII

ACTION THIS DAY

FIVE WEEKS after the Japanese surrendered and three months after the Labour Government won its first overall majority in Parliament, Graham Stainforth strode firmly between the rows of standing boys into prayers – which henceforth, he announced, would start two minutes early rather than two minutes late. This was an indication of the new Head's style, as Oundle was soon to learn.

Stern and forbidding in appearance, he seemed to embody the characteristics of a Victorian martinet. 'At their first encounter with him' Stainforth's obituary in the *Independent* noted, 'most parents, boys, staff and even governors probably felt awed or even a little frightened'. Considering his family background, this was not altogether surprising. His father was a Colonel in the Indian Army; four great grandfathers had been Generals. Indeed, but for bad eyesight he would probably have followed in their footsteps and become a General himself, like his brother. Instead he came to Oundle from Wellington.

Many Oundelians frankly admit that he scared them out of their wits. Others felt that he was rather a cold fish. Yet those who knew him better were aware that this intimidating cloak masked a man of sensibility and intellect. The glinting spectacles and the tight mouth hid a lively sense of mission and great moral courage; even the air of severity was belied by a twinkle of dry wit. 'That Rasputin of a priest', he once remarked of a highly respected cleric, 'Do you know what is wrong with that bishop? He's too full of the milk of human kindness.'

'But Graham,' his companion objected, 'I like bishops to be full of the milk of human kindness.'

'I didn't say that he was full of the milk of human kindness' replied Stainforth, 'I said that he was too full.'

As a critic, he was quick to spot weaknesses (after all it was part of his profession to do so) and he hated humbug or disloyalty. He could not abide 'behind the back' persons or anyone who failed to stand up and be counted if some vital issue was at stake. He was in no way devious and he stuck to his word, however caustically it was expressed. 'Some people were taught by him and never clicked with him' said his friend Sir Owen Chadwick. 'Many were taught by him in such a way that from Sydney to San Francisco they are still smiling at the memory, or imitating the rasp of his voice. He looked formidable. He sounded sometimes remote, especially when he wanted to sound remote. But behind that tremendous presence he cared about individual souls and their development'.

In short a headmaster, perhaps even a great headmaster, of the old school in a world that was evolving. It was a bold move by the governors to choose a man of this calibre – a distinguished teacher of English from a military background – to follow two scientists at Oundle. After the exhilarating expansion under Sanderson, and the lavish re-equipment under Fisher, they foresaw that the new headmaster would have to work under new and less favourable conditions. The postwar restrictions and inflation meant operating with limited resources, and making the best use of existing facilities. Worse still, the very concept of public schools was anathema to the government in power.

However, it soon became clear that Oundle was in the hands of a first class administrator. By sheer hard work, foresight, and a systematic approach to the most difficult of problems, and by redeploying and improving the existing fabric, Stainforth carried the school buoyantly through the troubled seas of rising prices, shortages and restrictive bureaucracy.

'I had no preconceived policies or ideas beyond sensing at my interview that the Governors considered there were no real Housemasters in the proper position, owing to Sanderson's deliberate dominance under which a man surrendered or left'. he wrote a few weeks before his death. 'In 1948 after more than two years I made some notes for myself:

a) The administration to be straightened out and made intelligent.

b) Housemasters to be stepped up first and then Prefects in whom latent leadership needs quickening to life.

c) The spirit as well as the machinery of the curriculum to be studied. Sanderson saw that Bach and Engineering could be made to serve a common end, but this in depth never got across.

d) It is clear that in him a great constructive genius had been at work – something big and adventurous and experimental and original had been attempted and partially carried through.

e) Only partially – and therefore the need was consolidation of which little was done in Fisher's time, hedged in as he was by monolithic Sanderson disciples. There was, therefore, a somewhat mechanical carrying on of Sanderson's work by a man with none of his genius, and I doubt if he put his finger on the weaknesses bequeathed by Sanderson.

f) Discipline: as I knew from Wellington, it was unfair to comment on this after six years of war and I found it offset by friendliness, overdrive, and an almost embarrassing loyalty by people eager for change. I found many of the best OOs were worried by the crudity of a lot of parents, their materialism, and the manners of the boys – too rich and without a sense of service and prefectorial responsibility and obligation.

'In a nutshell the task set me was to de-centralize, canalize and civilize.'

Consequently though the watchword of his regime was delegation of responsibility, Stainforth had first to move in what seemed to be the opposite direction. It was necessary for him to reorganize and strengthen the central administration, as well as rebuild the staff, before any of them could be given more individual responsibility.

'I'm glad, looking back, that I was comparatively young then,' says John Matthews, who rejoined the staff after war service in 1946. 'Some of my older colleagues found the pace often frenetic. I was amused to find that administration had more than a little of the military about it. Action this day! G.H.S. hadn't come from an army background for nothing. He also had a disconcerting habit of asking a head of department or the like for detailed plans for the next year or so. He himself referred to this habit in a staff meeting when he prefaced an announcement by saying: "Thinking ahead, as I sometimes do." That's still a catch phrase amongst my contemporaries, spoken if possible with that well-known rasp.'

It was fortunate for Stainforth that few entrenched conservatives were around who might have formed an organised opposition to the reforms he intended to introduce. Of the handful of men who had been young in the days of Sanderson when the place buzzed with new ideas, some were still teaching well. But the others had assumed the role of extinct volcanoes, uttering only an occasional objection that what was good enough for Sanderson was good enough for Stainforth. To these the response was crisp. One of them was told flatly that his tardiness in sending a return to the School Office was worse than the Civil Service. Within a year or two, moreover, some thirty new men were appointed to the staff and half the housemasterships fell vacant, enabling Stainforth to ease out those who had been appointed without tenure and to institute a fifteen-year limit.

His policy was to strengthen the position of the housemaster who – since the boys' academic progress rested in the hands of the form-masters – had become 'merely a kind of tutor'. Henceforth housemasters were to shoulder more of the responsibility for their charges' education and stop referring trivial matters to the School Office. To help them (and perhaps to forestall any criticism of his own Arts degree) Stainforth also appointed a scientific advisor, as well as an administrative assistant to look after all external and internal examinations. Various members of the staff were also delegated to fill other posts of a minor but essential character.

The time-table (with more than a hint of Sanderson about it) was modernised, and a master was put in charge of its implementation. In Fisher's day, as we noted, Oundle was accused of being far too orientated towards examinations ('a sausage machine for gaining certificates', an OO rather unfairly described it) and Stainforth's reforms, aided by the postwar certificate regulations, sought to correct any excess in this direction. But the drive for hard work and high achievement continued. Stainforth admired the vigour with which the average Oundelian tackled both work and play, an attitude he was determined to encourage. At the same time he set out to civilize it by placing a greater emphasis on the arts, and by stimulating the school's musical traditions.

Despite his autocratic manner, this spreading of responsibility succeeded. Housemasters and other key members of the staff began to take their own decisions and even question some of those that he made. It was a measure of this new confidence, and indeed his own flexibility, that one of the housemasters (whom he fondly called 'a loyal rebel') could return a memo with 'this is intolerable' scrawled over it, or that, having been icily cutting to another over the telephone, Stainforth could ring up again a few minutes later and admit that he had been wrong.

His job with the boys seemed at first to be contradictory. After the relaxed attitude that 'Bud' Fisher had adopted during the war (knowing that many of the older ones would soon be at what was called 'the sharp edge' and very likely on the Roll of Honour) it was necessary to reassert discipline and strengthen the prefectorial system, yet at the same time to liberalise and civilize the boys' conditions. Paradoxically, the two things went together. For while tightening up discipline he made it clear to the prefects, and through them to the whole school, that authority meant the spirit of leadership, indeed of public service, rather than just imposed obedience. This was, perhaps, a finical point to many boys, even if reinforced by his insistence on the importance to school life of the ideas underlying worship in Chapel (one of his 'liberal' edicts was that canings should be limited to six strokes – misses to count). But at the same time he tried to improve the general quality of life, which meant everything from brightening up corridors and classrooms to increasing the number of intellectual and cultural activities. Thus debating and other societies flourished; there were more lectures and expeditions. Conversaziones, which had been such an important feature in the pre-war era, became more wide-ranging and exciting than ever, and the academic syllabus was enlarged and geared less to pure success in examinations. An innovation was the NCE – one day each week on which there was No Compulsory Exercise.

A stick-and-carrot policy, if you like. But in practice it worked very well, and gradually Stainforth began to achieve a wider freedom of both opinions and actions within the school. On the one hand he made sure that the rules were firmly enforced – not only among the boys, but also the staff – which made him extremely unpopular at first. On the other, exceptions were constantly made for boys with particular interest. For instance, Sixth-formers went off unchaperoned to London for the day to a concert or an art gallery, and one sportsman still remembers the shock of being greeted during break by the headmaster saying: 'I hope you enjoyed the Huntingdon races yesterday.' Despite delegation, he knew what was going on.

As a former master recalls, Stainforth's presence was always there. 'Whenever one passed his study, even late at night, that stern face could be seen bent over the desk. He was at every school function, every major games fixture; he knew what all the school workmen were engaged in, and visited them regularly; every week he went to the sanatorium, the workshops, the laundry and the tuckshop. And yet his presence was stimulating, not inhibiting'.

Personally austere, he enjoyed other people's pleasures, and it may well be that in the process of civilising Oundle he allowed himself to be mellowed by the school. Certainly in his later years there were more activities, and less pressure: the school was more relaxed, with a lighter-hearted atmosphere that was epitomised by the regular masters' Review, 'Masterpieces', a show which was put on by Arthur Marshall and in which most of the teaching staff took part. The programme was kept a close secret, and in one finale Stainforth himself suddenly appeared, poking his head through a train window. He was wearing a loud cloth cap and scarf, and smoking a huge cigar. The well-known voice then rasped: 'How long am I to be kept waiting? This train is already fifteen and a half minutes late!'

After a stunned silence, the assembled school burst into cheers. Its formidable Head was now 'good old Gus'.

Arthur Marshall, who was then the Housemaster of New House, gave his own view of Stainforth's Oundle for the benefit of nostalgic OOs. It was entitled *"Plus ça change . . ."*

For those whose French never rose far above an uneasy year in B.2, the above quotation ends ". . . *plus c'est la même chose.*" You will have heard of new buildings and of old buildings refurbished and, in the case of the former Metal Shops, metallically gutted: you will have noted many changes in the Staff: you may even have heard of the Bursar's favourite *eau de Nil*, or Nile Water, paint which now graces so much of the beloved fabric, and OOs will be beginning to wonder if they would now be able to find their way from, say, Laxton to H.M.K's[1] old room. Well, you would. Everything is really very much as it was.

Let us make a short tour. Standing in the Cloisters, you would first be surprised/delighted/appalled to see ahead of you the only known Oundle attempt at a window-box, its green leaves (strangely like onions) full of promise for the Spring. Courage! Above this daring novelty can be seen the changeless head of F.T.J.,[2] either demonstrating upon the blackboard or engaged in constructive criticism with one of the livelier maths sets. To our left, unseen but splendidly audible, is A.C.C.,[3] upon the first floor (just about where Sgt. Crowley's rings were fixed) and explaining to V.B.2 just what a gerund is, while next door to him R.B.C.[4] is rattling through a *menu (vin compris)* which gave him pleasure in the Vosges in 1933, a pleasure heightened by many years of a plainer diet in one of the Oundle boarding houses. In the N.E. corner, smells, bangs and an occasional cheer show that the less elaborate labs are in full use. Gone for ever from the Cloisters are the whirr of the lathes, the whine from some refractory piece of metal, and the chug-chug of the engine in the S.E. corner, though other noises have replaced them – the steady drone from three new classrooms and the scratch of scraper-board, the hum of the pottery-apparatus, the click of the printing-press and the soft swoosh of rich gamboge on canvas, artistic activities taking place on the very spot where the experimental engine once stood.

Within the Cloisters, a light snowfall of sugar shows that buns are over. Part of G.W.B's[5] old room has been removed to form a cubby-hole-cum-oubliette for the School Porter, Batson. The original school office, which then became the Masters' Administration Centre (such confined quarters did not deserve the name Common Room) is now the province of the School Prefects. As in most schools, almost everything at Oundle used to be something else. The cloister notices show little that is new: so-and-so have their House colours: the following are

[1]King [2]Jackson [3]Cutcliffe [4]Cordukes [5]Brewster

to parade at the Armoury at 2 p.m.: only such-and-such have the right to walk across the Square: the Head of the School is highly displeased with certain untidy persons, and if this or that does not stop, there will be no more something or other till further notice: the School crew is going out at 2.45 (but from a different boat-house, and in an eight, and on a longer stretch of river).

Wherever our tour may take us from the Cloisters, the sights, sounds and smells are much the same. In Church Lane, once you have passed the customary click-clack through King's printing-shop window, you may have the good fortune to hear L.S.[1], from his nest in the upper region beyond the Brereton Room, giving Spanish or French tongue, or, nearby, the unison singing ('*Es war einmal ein Weihnachtsbaum*') of a German class led by W.Ct.[2] You would do well not to linger in Church Lane as L.S.'s method with books and other things that should not have been brought into the classroom has not changed with the years and you would hardly want to receive a Duncan and Starling upon the head.

Nearing the Gymnasium, cheerful shrieks may mean that P.T. has been temporarily abandoned for more stimulating net-ball: those who associate this game with girls' schools can draw what comfort they wish from the knowledge that it would be quite possible to get concussion during its rapid convolutions. Ahead of us is the Market Hall, inside which a former art master used to live, and hard by is the Bookshop, still one of our most attractive buildings, which now boasts display shelves groaning with more up-to-date literature than the *Tales from Shakespeare* and *Commonsense of the Calculus* upon the shelves behind.

Gone from its usual place near the fives courts is H.P.H.'s[3] patch of cabbages which used to scent so richly the Autumnal air while we watched the First XV making mincemeat of some visiting team. Some of us cannot look at the fives courts themselves without pleasantly visualising the School OTC Band of F.T.A.[4] resting within those shady recesses on hot days when their wind had given out. Grafton has sprouted a new wing, having been unable to arrange a Sidney fire, full of studies, a new library and places to wash: extra places to wash. Nestling in the trees between Sidney and Crosby, and overlooking the sacred stretch of B.V.K.'s[5] grass, stands a stoutly built bungalowette, the home of the new, and married, Crosby House-master, unmarried masters (can it be our bracing proximity to the East coast?) being now at a premium. Past the swimming-bath (most appreciated by the decreasing number of those who have once known the feel of Nene mud between their toes), and here is still the Armoury (shades of Puffer Irwin, The Major, and the day when a down-rifles-at-one o'clock-mutiny was happily averted by the simple plan of stopping parade at a reasonable time). The Armoury has thrown out a rash of new huts and shanties to house the complications of a modern army. Onto the Square, by way of the remainder game ground where Peter Scott used to keep a pet lizard inside his shirt when reluctantly forced to the wicket, and past the corner near those tall trees beneath which the band used so manfully to blow during the yearly Church Parade, to find

---

[1]Shaw [2]Cartwright [3]Hewett [4]Allen [5]Kingham

the nets, and a concrete wicket or two, and a Dutch barn, and the old and inadequate pavilion, now embellished with flower beds and rambling roses and, on occasion, a bellying canvas screen to protect adult bones from the worst from the North.

As 'Cabby' Marshall himself would have agreed, it was *la même chose* with a difference. The Stainforth era, especially in its later years, was a challenging and invigorating time for both masters and boys. Science and engineering thrived, biology expanded, the Workshops were concentrated on the Home Close along with a new foundry, and equipped with new machinery. On the arts side, the tempo was raised and fresh musical ideas were developed. Music scholarships improved the quality, and House competitions the quantity, in the individual use of instruments. Subscription concerts brought many renowned performers to Oundle, which stimulated School and House recitals. The Chancel Choir, the Male Voice Choir, the open air concerts, were all new initiatives. But the *oratorio*, with its thunderous non-choir passages sung by the whole school to point great moments, remained the characteristic product of Oundle music.

These years will be remembered for the B Minor Mass in floodlit Peterborough Cathedral; for the Coronation Tattoo and its Sabre jets and its Zulu assault on burning Rorke's Drift; for Tobias and his awe-inspiring Archangel; for the beating of the retreat by the white-gaitered new School Band.

And the sporting successes continued. After the great days of the Thirties it might have seemed difficult to maintain the same high standard of rugby football. Yet Oundle came to play an even larger part in the Cambridge side, and out of thirty post-war fixtures against other schools, the XV lost only two matches. 'Successful season ends great era at Oundle' was the headline in *The Times* when Frank Spragg finally retired after coaching the 1st XV for thirty-three years. 'In those years he has brought Oundle to a position which is almost unchallenged. For them to be beaten has been so rare as to be remarkable'. Indeed in eleven of those thirty-three seasons the XV was unbeaten, while in the last eleven years of his training no fewer than 53 matches were won out of 65 played, three were drawn, and only nine lost.

G.A. Wilson, who himself played for Oxford and won his cap for Scotland, remembers Spragg's insistence on team work, and his belief that because this could be developed by constant practice, the best football to play (and to watch) was school football. He recalls Spragg's ability to encourage without praising – a 20 point win would elicit the comment: 'Hmm, not bad'. On one occasion when Oundle were trailing badly in a school match, he strolled on to the field at half-time and spoke to the players, who proceeded to pulverise the opposition in the second half.

After the match a member of the XV was asked what magic words of wisdom Frank had offered to bring about such a transformation in the game. 'Nothing much,' came the reply. 'All he said was "if anyone sees the ball lying about I should pick it up if I were you."'

Cricket was much the same story under the guiding hands of Marcus Beresford and Michael Mills, who joined the staff in 1949. Uppingham remained the school to beat, and though this by no means always happened, Oundle's record in the scorebooks was still impressive. In athletics, too, most of the existing records were beaten; while Henley and Marlow had good reason to respect the School rowing eights.

During most of the Stainforth decade construction work was inhibited by restrictions and the lack of necessary permits. Indeed the only notable building to be erected during this period was the spacious new cricket pavilion which was paid for by OOs and opened by Queen Elizabeth the Queen Mother in 1956. (Its four dialled clock, incidentally, was built in the school workshops.) On the other hand an ambitious plan to spruce up the existing structures was carried out and, undeterred by bureaucratic obstruction, Stainforth and the Bursar, G.A. Rees, managed to improve many of them in the process. Thus Laxton School was remodelled with modern changing rooms and dining rooms; Grafton (which had not, like its sister Sidney, enjoyed the advantage of being gutted by fire) was brought up to modern standards by adding a wing of studies. Crosby, too, experienced the dubious pleasure of watching accommodation for a married housemaster sprout on its cherished lawn. The Bookshop was refurbished and a new Art Studio, with lemon, lime and scarlet wall, replace the old metal shops in the Cloisters. To relieve the congested Library, an ingenious new modern languages reading room was created, along with a Common Room for masters: rooms for teaching specialised subjects were fitted into old existing buildings.

All this represented a subtle shift away from the image Oundle had cultivated over the previous fifty years of being primarily an engineering school. Interpreting the governors' wishes, Stainforth widened the curriculum to place a greater emphasis on the Humanities. He wanted Oundle to offer a complete, rounded education; to be regarded as one of the great public schools and not a sort of junior polytechnic. Too many people, he said, believed that at Wellington everyone was always in uniform, and that Oundle was 'a kind of a garage'.

Scholarly and meticulous, he demanded high standards. Each notice he signed was carefully scrutinised, to the point that one master, tired of having his English corrected, consistently left out a comma so that honour could be satisfied on both sides by its restoration.

But he liked to be provocative, and his wit could be withering, as a parent discovered when he mentioned that he had been dining with the Duke of Airlie the previous night.

'You know him, of course?' the name-dropper added.

'No,' replied Gus. 'But you do, and that's obviously the main thing, isn't it?'

Like Samuel Butler, he was an Honest Man, and conscious of the fact. However, his inability to tell polite untruths led to some memorable sallies. When the school suffered from the disquisitions of a pompous adjudicator in a music competition, Stainforth's public comment was 'how much we enjoyed the adjudicator enjoying his adjudication'.

When the master in charge of athletics was being subjected to an inquisition about

Left *Queen Elizabeth the Queen Mother visited Oundle on 26 May 1956 for the celebrations of 400 years of the Schools' association with the Grocers' Company.*

something to do with his duties, he was goaded into exclaiming, 'Headmaster, I'm doing everything that's humanly possible.' To which Stainforth replied 'But that's not enough!', and burst out laughing.

He could also tell a story against himself. At the start of an end of term speech, he related how an Old Boy had been strolling along the street with his wife when he saw the headmaster approaching on the other side. 'Good heavens,' the chap whispered to her, 'there's bloody old Gus! Let's nip into that shop to avoid him.'

But it was too late, and so they went over. As they shook hands, the Old Boy said suavely: 'I want you to meet my wife. I was just saying to her "How lucky, there's Mr Stainforth. Let's go over and have a word with him."'

'You said nothing of the sort,' replied Stainforth. 'What you said was "Good heavens, there's bloody old Gus. Let's nip into that shop and avoid him."'

His sermons in chapel were pithy and to the point. In those days there was evensong on Sundays in addition to mattins. One evening John Matthews was reading the lesson when all the lights went out. Fortunately it was a familiar passage and he was able to continue until they came on again. As he passed the Headmaster's stall a gritty voice muttered: 'Next time you'd better memorise the whole lesson.'

On another occasion the same housemaster received a memo from the Head and dropped his answer into the box outside the Headmaster's study on his way to a lecture. After the lecture, he went into the Masters' Common Room before returning to the House. When he got back his wife told him that Stainforth had phoned to speak about the memo. She had replied that we was at the lecture. 'But that,' came the icy retort, 'was twenty minutes ago.'

Even his wife Ruth, who sustained him so well, was apt to poke fun about his irritation at any delay. When driving in France they were held up by a lumbering lorry which would not pull out of the way however frantically he hooted. 'Obviously,' she murmured, 'he does not realise that you are the Headmaster of Oundle.'

Clearly he believed that Oundle responded best to a foot planted firmly on the accelerator. And he stood on the gas with militant efficiency. At heart he was less of an academic than a top grade staff officer. Under different circumstances he might have made an excellent Chief of Imperial General Staff. As it was, he became Oundle's 'Monty'. (The Field Marshal and Gus had much in common. They certainly shared the same ruthless drive.)

At the age of 83, a bent old man virtually destroyed by the death of his beloved Ruth, he could still sum up much of the substance of this book in a few characteristic phrases:

'Three great figures in the public school world' he said, 'all came from the Midlands. Arnold, who was appointed to save the public schools, full of vice and indifference and bullying. He created a lot of prigs, but they went out to serve the Empire (*vide* Indian Civil). Thring created the HMC (Head Masters' Conference) and – partly through games – also established the public schools as producing men who were shareholders in Victorian prosperity with a sense of service and feudal obligation.

'Sanderson reacted against that and aimed at developing men for a world which he sensed was changing – which is why H.G. Wells fell for him. Neither was a 'gentleman' nor a believer in the feudal status quo – leadership and an 'officer class'. And that was why I believe Oundle was different. The charge against me could be that I tried – and to some extent succeeded – in making it the same.'

In *Life's Rich Pageant* Arthur Marshall paid him this tribute: 'He did great good and rates the highest marks.' To which Michael Mills adds: 'You can say what you like, but he was a great and perceptive person to serve under.'

By 1956 there were more boys in the school than ever before – 666 in Stainforth's final term (the number, as he delightedly pointed out, of the Beast in *Revelation*). Aware that much remained to be achieved, he nevertheless resigned to become Headmaster of his old school, Wellington. While at Oundle, he was a member of the Oxford and Cambridge Joint Examination Board, and Chairman of the Joint Standing Committee of the Headmasters Conference and the IAPS. But as he said, ten years is enough for any man in any institution. 'If you haven't done what you want to do in ten years, you'll never do it.' And when consulted by the Governors, he gave as a prescription for his successor: 'Someone who isn't so keen on the bumph, and is a scholar.'

The Grocers' Company paid him the compliment of appointing such a man.

XIII
MODIFYING RIGID PATTERNS
OUNDLE UNDER DICK KNIGHT

I F STAINFORTH was faced with a problem of reorganisation, his successors had to deal with a social problem. Dick Knight became headmaster of Oundle at the height of the Suez crisis in 1956, just as the last nail was being knocked into the coffin of Britain's imperial saga.

At the time, Suez seemed a blunder. In retrospect, it was a folly. Not only did it make Nasser the darling of the non-aligned world and enabled him to export his revolution, but it discredited the Old Guard at home and destroyed a number of sacred cows in the process. By the Sixties practically everything that stood for authority – Government, the Law, the Church – was being derided by the coming generation. Parents and conventional morality were flouted. Even God was scorned.

This satirical irreverence was perhaps an inevitable backlash in the transition from Great Britain to Little England. Harold Macmillan might speak of 'the winds of change' and reiterate the slogan 'You've never had it so good'. Yet nothing could disguise the sense of social malaise that was sweeping through the country.

Yes, the 'swinging Sixties' were a confusing, sweet-sour decade – a curious mixture of decadence and idealism. Often it seemed as though the collective aggression of the imperial epoch was being transformed by the young into a debased violence. In fact the conflict was less of a political expression than a confrontation between youth and age. It was, if you like, a clash between a generation that had no experience of fighting a war and its parents who knew what they had been fighting about. Young people with money to burn sought to eradicate the barriers of class and nationality; united together by a pop culture that excluded their elders, they rejected the compromises and hypocricies of the adult word. At the same time some of them exploited the idea of a permissive society by indulging in an orgy of drugs, sex, and violence.

The youth revolt sparked off what Dr John Rae, headmaster of Taunton and then Westminster, called the 'public school revolution' – the title he gave to an incisive and brilliant book which examined how the changes and attitudes in the country affected public schools. Obviously as traditional establishments exercising authority over the young, such schools were bound to be regarded as an offensive anachronism by those with radical ideas. But in addition to public criticism they were faced with the threat of political action after Harold Wilson's election victory in 1964. It was undoubtedly a difficult time.

Granted, the public schools had experienced similar criticism and threats in the past.

There had been plans afoot to reform them even before the war. E.C. Mack believed that the most likely solution (if there was to be one at all) would be for them to accept state interference and admit into their ranks the best element of the working class. He thought that the public schools should reform in the direction of liberal working class aims, whilst remaining at least semi-independent boarding schools with an emphasis on 'training for leadership'.

Published in 1941, Mack's book *The Public Schools and British Opinion* reflected the general feeling that the public schools would inevitably have to reform or die. Indeed at the HMC's request, the President of the Board of Trade, R.A.Butler, asked Lord Fleming to set up a committee to consider how the public schools could be brought closer into the county's educational system.

The Fleming Report of 1944 recommended that 25 per cent of the intake should be made available to non-paying pupils through the Board of Education and local education authorities. But no one showed any inclination to put the scheme into practice.

'I think that if a Conservative government had won the General Election of 1945 something on the lines of the Fleming scheme would have started,' says Sir Robert Birley, a member of the Committee. 'If so, I think that by now it would be regarded as quite commonplace. I think the scheme would not have destroyed the independence of the public schools. However, Labour won the Election of 1945. They were not opposed to the scheme in principle. But they were not prepared to have a scheme run under the Ministry and the Treasury: the whole thing was to be run by the Local Education Authorities. As soon as I heard of this decision, I realised the scheme was doomed.'

Labour had always seen the public schools as enemies to be destroyed. If this hatred was not translated into immediate action, it was because the Attlee administration had more pressing priorities to deal with. However, by 1955 the Party, then in opposition, was firmly resolved to absorb the grammar schools into a new comprehensive system. This was to be their first step when they returned to power. But by improving their academic standards the public schools were already 'creaming' off the brightest pupils and thus posing a threat to the comprehensive schools which could not be ignored.

When Harold Wilson's Government came into office in 1964, it was with the declared intention of tackling the problem. Antony Crosland, the Secretary of State for Education (and an Old Wykehamist) appointed a commission 'to advise on the best way of integrating the public schools with the state system of Education'. Yet even such a direct challenge did not bring about the result that socialist critics had hoped for. The Commission's first report concentrated on boarding schools. Helped by the research of a young sociologist who had never himself been a boarder, it concluded that its objectives would be achieved by making public schools give half their places to some 80,000 children from poor homes. In this way they would cease to be socially divisive and become more academically comprehensive. In effect, they would be integrated without being abolished.

Once again the plan of action met with little enthusiasm. Whereas Labour left-wingers had no desire to see them escape by donning egalitarian colours, the moderates were daunted by the sheer cost of such a cumbersome operation. They realised, too, that the demand for boarding school education came chiefly from middle-class parents. The Commission therefore shifted its attention to the direct grant schools – such as Manchester Grammar, King Edward's, Birmingham, Oakham and so forth – which, by the Education Act of 1902, received financial support from the government in return for giving places to bright pupils from state primary schools. Though intended to be a path to opportunity for children from modest homes, the direct grant schools were now regarded as socially divisive because they were academically selective.

The Commission's recommendations came as no surprise. The direct grant was to cease; schools which had received them could choose between joining the comprehensive system or becoming fully independent. But when Wilson's second administration abolished the direct grant in 1975, the result was less predictable. Of the 178 schools involved, 119 chose to remain outside the state system, thereby swelling the ranks of the independents – which was not quite what Labour intended.

Moreover some of them were highly successful: Oakham, for instance, which had been the grammar school for Rutland since 1946. Returning to independent status the school embarked on a massive expansion programme under John Buchanan, building nine new houses for day pupils and boarders, a new junior school, a sports complex, a swimming pool and design centre. This expansion paved the way for admitting girls, thirty of whom made their first appearance in the sixth from. Their numbers increased until the school had become more or less coeducational. (Today, with 936 pupils in the junior and senior schools, 539 are boarders and 397 day pupils, the ratio being 439 girls to 497 boys.) In the words of the present headmaster, Graham Smallbone, 'Over the past twenty years Oakham has changed dramatically, coeducation being the biggest change'. In fact, since losing its grant, Oakham has developed into a dynamic public school. A remarkable outcome! But it does not alter the fact that for over twenty years the future of the public schools was a controversial issue, and that after 1963 the *mot* in scholastic circles was that all schools were either 'comprehensive or apprehensive'. However, when R.J.Knight arrived at Oundle in 1956 the public school revolution had not yet started, and the framework of compulsion that controlled the lives of Oundelians was still unchanged. Knight came from Marlborough, where a high degree of consultation existed between headmaster and staff. 'At Oundle I found a school tightly structured, with a degree of centralisation which I thought a bit extreme,' he recalls. 'All entries made through the headmaster's office, all university applications channelled through him, and so on. The 'head of steam' was notorious and impressive, and there was a fine sense of pride and achievement, albeit on a slightly restricted field'. 'A' level results were excellent, university entrance scholarships slightly less so – 7 in 1956, compared with the Marlborough norm of 12.

'The rugger record was embarrassingly good: Oundle had not lost a school match for two years (and not lost to Stowe for over twenty years). Fives was first-rate, squash non existent, cricket moderate. The oarsmen had just had an *annus mirabilis*, reaching the Henley final; hockey was scarcely played. Music was superb, but inevitably tended to concentrate on the annual 'whole school' performance. Drama laboured under the handicap of having no proper stage, but was doing pretty well on the one specially erected in the Great Hall each spring. There was a highly complicated system of 'colours' and awards, usually presented in public on the lawn after chapel. Beating and fagging were still in operation, though – like most things – under efficient housemagisterial control. It was a matter of pride in some quarters that hip-baths were still in use. The boys were almost unanimously proud and delighted with their school and its triumphs; and the quater-centenary celebrations of 1956 with the Queen Mother's visit that June seemed to bring a memorable era to an end.'

More stylish than Fisher, less ruthless than Stainforth, R.J. Knight was a brilliant classical scholar and an athlete of note. Educated at Dulwich and Trinity College, Cambridge, he had been appointed to his new position from being a housemaster at Marlborough.

Everyone liked Knight, even his critics, and everyone called him 'Dick'. A good administrator with a firm grasp of the school's material needs, he nevertheless preferred the personal touch to dealing with paperwork. His role, as he saw it, was to keep the place humming but at the same time to encourage more self questioning, and to offer a greater variety of outlets for boys who were not naturally gifted in Oundle's traditional activities.

He was determined to raise academic standards and to root out the illiterate scientist or the innumerate historian. 'Coming from Marlborough where in those days the tide ran strongly to classics and history, I was familiar with the need to induce intelligent historians to take science seriously,' he explained. 'At Oundle the tide tended to run the other way, and most intelligent boys went to the Science Sixth forms. This meant that at both schools it was often the boy of real character who would resist the tide and choose the less popular course – and have to justify his choice to his friends. Certainly there were several extremely able historians, economists, and classicists at the top of the school whom it was often quite hard to persuade that science had anything for them. Minority subjects are notoriously difficult to teach well to a group of pupils whose main interest lies elsewhere, and competent teachers are primarily interested in their own specialists.

'However, we did keep a minority time course of something like a quarter of the timetable for subjects other than those taken to 'A' level. A little French or Latin – later Russian, – a general studies course including a weekly lecture from some distinguished visitor. There were also the Industry links. I so well remember George Woodcock as a house guest, not to mention Geoffrey Crowther, Group Captain Cheshire, and of course Monty, Trevor Huddleston, and other controversial folk. I also remember Humphrey Littleton giving a concert on the same Sunday as his former headmaster at Eton, Robert Birley, had been preaching in Chapel. Two little attempts to introduce the outside world to Oundle were exchange visits with a North London comprehensive, and a parallel arrangement with a Cologne gymnasium.

'This rather inadequate diet was all we managed to provide for the opportunities for cross-fertilisation of ideas which I knew ought to characterise a lively Sixth form.'

The need to correct the notorious narrowness of Sixth form work was becoming generally accepted by educational authorities. But Oundle was one of the first schools to sign ABC (the Agreement to Broaden the Curriculum) and thus ensure that at least 25% of a Sixth former's time was taken up with non-specialist studies. The Block system, evolved from a working paper produced by the Schools' Council in 1966, was promptly introduced; this meant that hitherto unavailable combinations of main subjects were now offered. Boys could choose an option from each of the three main subject Blocks (A,B, and C) together with non-specialist subjects from Blocks D and E.

BLOCK A 8 periods	BLOCK B 8 periods	BLOCK C 8 periods	BLOCK D 6 periods	BLOCK E 6 periods
Mathematics	Physics	Mathematics	Projects	Divinity
Physics	Chemistry	Biology	(a triple period)	plus
Chemistry	English	Economics	plus	Language Sets
English	Geography	Political Science	Use of English	
History	German	French		
	Spanish	Latin		
	Greek			

Once this system was adopted, the old form structure disappeared. No longer was there a Classical Sixth, a Modern Sixth, a History Sixth, or a variety of Science Sixths. Instead the whole Sixth form was listed in tutorial groups, with a master – usually a specialist in the main subject – allotted to each group. This 'tutor' replaced the old form master, and organised the end of term reports.

Lower down the school, the old rigid pattern was also modified. True, Dick Knight was a cautious innovator, who eschewed change for its own sake. But he was always willing to experiment, and he felt that the curriculum for new entrants was absurdly out-of-date. Though the new boy had done no science at his prep school, the policy was still to give him only the merest smattering in his first year, while he took 'O' levels (at the age of 13 or 14) in the traditional prep school subjects – that is, English, Latin, Geography, History, Maths, French. Those with a scientific bent could then say farewell to such matters for ever, while being force-fed with Physics and Chemistry in the hope of getting three good 'A' level grades by the time they were sixteen – which left two or even three years to gain admission to the science faculties of a university.

This was now changed. Instead, on arrival, all boys were compelled to take two years to their first 'O' levels, and to study at least two sciences at proper depth before making their choice of 'A' level subjects. It was not until later, under Dr Trapnell, that the Fifth forms were re-organised into a Block system similar to that operating in the Sixth.

But Dick Knight did more than adjust the curriculum. His tenure was marked by a string of projects made possible by the Appeal which was launched in November 1957 and achieved its quarter-million target in 1960.

Chronologically, the first new building to appear was the Palmer Chemistry Block on the Home Close in 1958. This was named after H.C. Palmer, the senior chemistry master who had been appointed by Sanderson and was still teaching when Knight arrived. Flanking it was the Lyons Memorial Lecture Room, donated by Sir William Lyons, the founder and Chairman of Jaguar cars, in memory of his only son, John, who was tragically killed in a road accident near Rouen while driving a C Type to Le Mans.

In 1960 the old wooden Art Studio (which had formerly been the Engine Shop) was pulled down, and the whole East side of the Cloisters redesigned to provide new classrooms, a history library, and more modern Art Rooms. Next came the 'North Street Refectory' with its kitchen and dining halls for three of the town houses – Bramston, Laundimer, and the Berrystead – which were at the same time modernised: extra studies and recreational facilities were provided in the old dining rooms and kitchens (often in the basement) while central heating did away with the problems of carrying coal.

The Great Hall gallery was extended to give room for seventy extra seats; the Chapel organ was reconstructed and endowed with a new console; the Music School was enlarged. In 1962, partly because of the frustration caused by contractors' delays and partly to save money, the new Bursar, Gim Milton, proposed that his own augmented labour force should tackle the subsequent projects.

It was a timely suggestion, and the next few years saw the completion of the splendid new Cripps Library (the first gift of a family which was to become one of the School's most generous benefactors) above the Cloisters; the new Geography Department; the Field House Refectory with new dining halls for Laxton and Crosby, and the subsequent modernisation of these two early 'hostel-type' houses through imaginative use of the space released by the removal of cooking and eating areas.

Three squash courts were built on the Home Close in 1965. In the same year John Piper redesigned the East end of the Chapel. The Bookshop in the Market Place was extended and brought up to date; in the dedicated hands of Juliet Russell it was to become well-known to bibliophiles. Also in Knight's time a new language laboratory and a planning centre for the Workshops materialised, while the Mathematics Library and Laboratory of 1966 witnessed a tentative introduction of work with computing and data-processing as well as some electronics projects in what had been the old Pattern Shop.

On the sporting side, it would have been over-sanguine to hope that the rugger record

The Old Cripps Library was one of several building projects initiated by Dick Knight in the early Sixties. The splendid New Cripps library, originally the old School Gymnasium, was opened in April 1988.

would stand unblemished after the heyday of the 'Spragg era', though Oundle still won more matches than it lost. And the Henley results from 1956-59 were something of a flash in the pan. On the other hand cricket improved greatly. Hockey began to take off, and there was a growth of interest in the less competitive sports such as sailing, mountaineering and canoeing. In Norway a group of twenty boys in full kit marched 100 miles in four days; in 1966 the relay team swam the Channel in such appalling weather conditions that even the press covering the event went home.

Equally, the CCF (Combined Cadet Force) was as keen as ever, while music and drama occupied more boys than before and produced some outstanding performances. Though such yardsticks should be viewed with caution, there is no denying that the twelve Oxford and Cambridge awards obtained in 1966 seemed to confirm that the academic side of the school was sound.

Unhappily this is more than could be said of the outside world. In 1963 the Beatles lifted the lid and gave youth a rallying point against authority just before the Wilson Government came into office apparently hellbent on destroying the public schools. So in one way or another prospects must have looked gloomy to any headmaster. 'It was an appalling period,' says John Matthews, who was then Second Master at Oundle. 'Everything was questioned.'

Yet Dick Knight does not appear to have been unduly disturbed. Unlike some other heads, he did not lose his nerve; little notice was taken at Oundle of the controversy over public schools, since the place was exceedingly popular in the areas where it mattered – that is,

Above Dick Knight, Viscount Montgomery of Alamein, and 'top brass' on the River Nene at Tanser in 1960.

among potential parents and the OO fraternity. He himself was more concerned with keeping the school numbers within bounds (thereby causing a good deal of unpopularity with OOs who had failed to register their sons in time). Occasionally, of course, the staff were aware of criticism, chiefly on the ground of 'elitism' and 'selectiveness by the purse'. But on the whole they felt it best to get on with the job.

The return of the Labour Government certainly brought this issue to the forefront, and the Public Schools Commission of 1965 did its best to make sensible proposals about integration. Three members of the Commission spent some time at Oundle. But it was soon obvious that short of abolition (which in effect meant the making of fee-charging for education illegal) there was no way forward. So eventually the Socialists turned their attacks to easier targets such as the direct grant schools.

'I think it is fair to say that there were a good many headmasters of that period who would have welcomed closer links with the maintained system. Certainly I would have done so,' Knight comments. 'But such pipe-dreams foundered on the rocks of financial stringency. It costs a good deal to educate a boy or girl well, and it is really unrealistic to expect anyone but the parents to bear the brunt of this expense. As to the suggestion that we were amateurish or ineffective – I can't remember hearing it. Such comments as came my way from the outer world rather indicated that we were too effective, an object of jealousy. Admittedly Oundle may have been a bit special, with its reputation for science orientation, and absence of what might be called toffee-nose. Laxton School, I suppose, helped locally.'

For all this, Oundle did tend to lag behind the times in certain of its customs, and some liberalisation was clearly needed even without pressure from outside. The Oundelian regime was still pretty spartan, and probably more monastic than desirable. Less permissive in dress than many other schools, it was also reluctant to introduce such innovations as a Sixth form bar. Likewise it was rigidly opposed to smoking, and permitted only prefects to ride bicycles. Contacts with the opposite sex were left to the holidays; in term time even dances were a rarity. Though Oundle was never a particularly 'pious' school, the puritan spirit evidently still lingered on.

Throughout the Knight era, however, there was a steady easing of the old rigid traditions. Demarcation rules in houses were relaxed; inter-house visits were allowed; more fraternising between staff and pupils was encouraged. Dress regulations were simplified (not least for the sake of economy) and green sports jackets replaced the uniform dark grey Daniel Neale suits. The two-compulsory-chapels-a-Sunday pattern was modified so as to be more in tune with the times. The long-established 'Workshops Week', which gave boys a break from normal work and an unbroken session in one of the 'shops', was kept; but older pupils were allowed, indeed encouraged, to spend their week doing a project outside the workshops, provided that it was monitored by a master. The CCF became optional for senior boys if they

Left *Oundle's cross channel swimmers begin their battle against atrocious conditions in a relay race in late July 1966. Six boys covered the distance from Cap Gris Nez to St Margaret's Bay in 11 hours, 45 minutes.*

selected an alternative activity. As a result the Social Service Unit, inaugurated as early as 1958, became popular as an opportunity to help elderly or disadvantaged people.

As always, of course, there were a few who pushed to see how far they would be permitted to go. Irritation was caused by boys reluctant to kneel in Chapel or say the Creed ('And why should they,' the headmaster was heard to ask, 'if they don't believe it?'); by others who protested against the athletics cult, as they saw it, by walking away while 'colours' were being awarded in public; by one boy's refusal to take the Scout Oath – though there was some uncertainty whether it was loyalty to the Queen or to God that he was loath to admit. 'A particular problem,' Dick Knight recalls, 'arose in the early Sixties over the wearing of the CND badge, very much in vogue just then among students. It was argued that as Scout badges had long been admissible, it was illogical to ban others. For a short time they were allowed – even the Head of School appeared with one. But it was soon decided that comments from visitors made it impossible to countenance this degree of freedom.'

If CND badges were not countenanced, there was at least a move to do away with two of the most notorious features of public school life. Thus, following a general (and admirable) trend, fagging by one boy for another was replaced by community chores, while beating by prefects quietly – though not entirely – died out.

On the other hand drugs, which were beginning to cause serious concern in the country as a whole, and indeed in some schools nearer London, do not seem to have worried the Oundle authorities until after 1968. Perhaps the school was fortunate in its rural location; perhaps more went on than was unearthed. At any rate rule-breakers, and those who tried to catch them, were more concerned with alcohol and tobacco than anything more lurid.

Later, during Dr Trapnell's time, there were a couple of incidents which resulted in the expulsion of the boys concerned – one who had apparently brought some marijuana from abroad, another who seems to have been given it by his parents . . . Of course boys are secretive about such matters. However, the Head of School told me an amusing if apocryphal little story about a boy in Laundimer who handed his housemaster a plant in a pot, asking him to water it for him during the holidays. This the housemaster was good enough to do, and handed it back to him at the beginning of the next term – never realising that it was a cannabis plant.

That is about as far as the drug culture went in Oundle, which on the whole survived the youth revolution without much serious unrest. But this does not mean that it was always an easy passage. 'As captain of the ship Dick Knight had to involve himself below decks and keep a check on the tiller because of the choppy waters of social change, rather than studying the charts and deciding the route the ship was to take,' comments Roger Freebairn, who had been a boy under Stainforth and returned to teach English under Knight. 'Gus could tell the steerer where to take the ship. Dick had to deal with each development on an *ad hoc* basis.'

Even so, Knight liked to claim that the Oundelian of the mid-Sixties was more adult than his forebears. 'He was more earnest, willing to work harder for an acknowledged goal, perhaps more impatient of subjects, approaches, even traditions, whose value was not immediately apparent.'

An irksome rule was not so often broken in a spirit of devil-may-care as seriously challenged in an attempt to get it amended. A master who was casual or inept was no longer a figure of fun and popularity, but despised as wasting valuable time. Another feature of adulthood is sympathy, and he was always struck by the real sense of responsibility shown by prefects towards the weaker and less competent new boy. Bullying, no doubt, survived in dark corners. But he genuinely believed that the unhappy small boy was far less a feature of Oundle than in Knight's own schooldays.

These sentiments seem to sum up the philosophy of education which he tried to follow. Clearly his greatest single problem was the reluctance of an intelligent and articulate minority to accept compulsion or indeed responsibility of any sort (and in some cases even to reject the system while demanding its benefits as a right). Personal freedom had to be extended without the appearance of retreating under pressure; a good deal of patience had to be exercised while the liberating reforms were gradually introduced. At times, for all his friendliness, Knight's temper could flare at the scent of what the army would call 'dumb insolence'. One of his last senior prefects recalls an incident involving severe punishment of a large group of boys for quite a trivial offence, and though Dick now prefers not to remember the matter, he confesses that it may have occurred. To such lengths, he adds wryly, can the mildest of men be driven.

But whatever the reason, it is certain that none of the anti-establishment feelings boiled over at Oundle, as they sometimes did elsewhere. For this, some credit is due to Knight's enlightened regime, and to the excellent appointments he made to the staff. He left a more cheerful, and numerically a larger community than he had inherited, of 741 pupils. There was, indeed, a general sense of regret when he announced that he had accepted a new appointment as headmaster of Monkton Combe.

'He was a delightful man to work with,' says John Matthews, 'he raised academic standards and abolished a lot of pettifogging rules. But the school was difficult to handle and he lacked that streak of ruthlessness that every headmaster should have.'

Into this arena of potential resentment stepped B.M.W. Trapnell in the autumn of 1968, a particularly sensitive moment in public school history.

XIV

GLASNOST AND COMPUTERS

'A YEAR OR TWO before I arrived at Oundle, the Head of School – a concerned and sensitive boy, now in orders – found to his distress that it was his duty to cane thirty-eight boys who had walked into chapel with their suit jackets unbuttoned,' remarked Barry Trapnell recently. 'This sad and irritating incident symbolises how the desire of the young for less authoritarianism, let's say for more acceptance of them as individuals, was ending in a divisive triviality – and diverting attention from the more important issues of the time.'

Of these, most serious of all perhaps, was that society had been virtually static for years, and the middle classes still thought that the system would carry them along. But suddenly a whole series of issues cropped up which did not fit into that system.

On the one hand young people at independent schools had to make their own way along the lines that society wanted, which meant passing 'A' levels. It also involved them in being trained for leadership at a time when leadership posts were no longer waiting for them. On the other, there was the style of leadership itself, which made many of the young feel uneasy. They were reluctant to become part of a separate authoritarian sect. They wanted a more open situation.

They found their parents baffled by the sexual revolution. Why, boys asked themselves, should the relationship between the sexes be taboo and closed? Why should they not be allowed to dress as they pleased and grow their hair as long as they liked? To the young, short hair was identified with the adult world, with the military and the police, with what was called 'square'. In contrast, long hair was seen as a gesture of individuality – and, paradoxically, as a communal badge in the rebellion against convention. Flowing locks suggested artiness rather than heartiness.

The generation of the late Sixties and early Seventies believed that their life styles and values, their attitudes and culture, should be more free and easy, more indulgent. They felt that anything which appeared to be closed should be opened. Pop music was their symbol centre, and the lyrics of the group King Crimson were practically a rallying call. The stones on which the prophets wrote are cracking at the seams.

For any new headmaster, the challenge was to try to keep a sense of solidarity. True, there was bound to be a latent hostility between boys and masters, a 'Them-and-Us' feeling which could not be entirely removed. But such polarisation had to be avoided as far as possible. It was necessary to try and sympathise with youth's aspirations without capitulating.

'Leadership styles vary between the aloof demigod and the superchum,' explained Barry Trapnell. 'I was not a particularly chummy chap about the place. I wanted to be a human being – but time was precious and there's always a difficult decision about how a head's activities should be allocated. To speak in caricature terms, the difficulty was how to deal with features reminiscent of a concentration camp without ending up with a Butlin's, while simultaneously attempting to decide what new features in the school life might help to prepare the young for their later lives'.

Off duty, Barry Trapnell is informal and jolly. He exudes bonhomie. His conversation is stimulating and epigrammatic. He might be taken for a high-ranking EEC administrator, perhaps, or an intellectual industrialist. The last thing you would imagine is that this was the formidable headmaster who took Oundle to the top rank of independent schools in the 16 years between 1968 and 1984, in so doing adding a new dimension to British education.

Dr B.M.W. Trapnell had been a scholar at University College School, London, and St John's College, Cambridge. He was successively a research student under Sir Eric Rideal (himself an OO) and at Northwestern University near Chicago, a don at Oxford, a university lecturer at Liverpool, a consultant to ICI and various American oil companies in the States. He wrote numerous papers for learned journals, a study, *Chemisorption* (which was translated into Russian and Polish), and an SPCK paperback entitled *Learning and Discerning in Higher Education*. He played cricket, squash and fives for Cambridge; cricket for the Gentlemen and for Middlesex; squash for Middlesex; and won the Amateur Fives Championships three times. He became a connoisseur of silver and ceramics, and travelled to Orrefors to investigate Swedish glass. He sits on a number of boards, is a lay reader and was Deputy Lieutenant of Staffordshire. An impressive c.v., though he had never worked in a school, save as a day-boy and as a headmaster: he put Denstone on the map before coming to Oundle.

It is perhaps surprising that the governors should have chosen a man with such unusual credentials. But the Grocers like an alternation in their heads between 'insane innovators' and 'sane consolidators'. Having had three of the latter in succession, they selected Barry for the former role.

Sanderson had been an innovator. Fisher a consolidator. Stainforth had tightened things up; Dick Knight had carried them on. So, after this long period of consolidation, and, at the height of the youth movement, Trapnell 'lit the blue touch paper', and the fireworks followed.

'Public schools had become inappropriate,' he says. 'They needed to be reviewed. A new era was coming to birth. There was no God-given right any longer, and since you couldn't rely on His support any more you had to get on your bike and start pedalling. The inward-looking nature of most schools had been allowed to carry on too long. An unchallenged mystique! And the time had come to challenge it.'

Which was precisely what Dr Trapnell proceeded to do. Having been a don and a business executive, but never a schoolmaster, he adopted the role of managing director, or rather executive chairman, since the Oundle Committee was content to act as watch-dog without actually interfering. His style was that of a business chief who wanted action and not amiable chat. Purposeful chats were encouraged, to be sure, and he always found time for boys who had problems, but he preferred the staff to give answers to the propositions that were put forward. He worked in a purposeful fashion, setting up policy committees of masters, or committees of prefects, and usually accepting their recommendations.

His first act was to amplify the block system which had been started under Dick Knight for pupils taking 'A' levels, and which had become more or less universal in all schools. This he now introduced into the Fifth forms at Oundle which were sitting for 'O' levels, with a corpus of English/French/Maths/Physics/Chemistry, once again with a third of the teaching week kept for a choice of other subjects.

Previously, as we know, form masters looked after whole forms. But with the arrival of the block system, tutors took over, and this situation was catalysed by bringing in the Fifth forms as well. The tutorial system was therefore extended to cover the entire school.

Hitherto, the Houses had been run by their housemasters with the help of a resident bachelor tutor. Now, each House was allocated three other masters, all of them acting as tutors. As a result, every tutor took charge of a fifth of the house. His primary duty was to look after each of these boys, keeping a close eye on his academic progress and extra-curricular activities, advising on subject choices, university entrance or career, and so forth. The effect of the tutorial system was to reduce the housemaster's load, and involve almost everyone in house life.

Giving boys a feeling that the school was seeking to do its best for them as individuals, was an important innovation. What is more, it filled the vacuum which arose when forms ceased to exist in the old fashioned sense, and a form master could no longer guide classes of boys academically.

'So we replaced them by a system whereby virtually all the staff were attached to houses to act as tutors,' explains Barry. 'The tutor's primary function was to oversee the whole progress, academic and extra-curricular, of thirteen or fourteen members of the house. But he was also responsible for an evening duty each week, and was expected to assist with house activities such as games and drama. In this way, the house became a mini-college, a kind of extended family, rather than – to use the language of caricature again – the territory of housemaster-barons, with the rest of the staff almost irrelevant pastorally. A more personal supervision of boys was engendered, and a greater togetherness of the school community.'

Academically, too, the effects of this change were stimulating. For eight successive years the examination results steadily improved, reaching the remarkable figures of 87.3% 'O' level passes, and at 'A' level 89.7%, which meant that Oundle was consistently placed among the top four or five independent schools.

But the school also scored an academic breakthrough in another way, and that was by exploiting 'the creative possibilities of the new'. For the recent discovery of the silicon chip was an epic advance – comparable in importance with the invention of the wheel, or the Industrial Revolution – and Dr Trapnell was determined that Oundle should take the lead in this exciting new technology. By 1974 there was already a successful electronics side, which was experimenting with basic components, and indeed the school began the construction of a micro-computer to its own design. From this grew the idea of establishing a full micro-electronics laboratory.

The brainchild of two masters, John Coll and Charles Sweeten, it was 'net-worked' – that is, roughly speaking, twelve computers joined together – and was as such the first in any school, either in Britain or abroad. Thus Oundle became a pioneer in the introduction of micro-electronics. Two successive Secretaries of State, Mark Carlisle and Sir Keith Joseph, came to see for themselves what the school was doing; and over eleven hundred institutions – independent and maintained schools, colleges of Further and Higher Education, Polytechnics and universities both in Britain and overseas – came and sought information and help.

Many schools found it difficult, if not impossible, to incorporate micro-electronics into an already full timetable. But at Oundle the Workshops Week enabled this new subject to be added to the curriculum as an option. Consequently any boy in the school could choose to receive instruction which allowed him to learn how to operate and programme computers; and by using the basic training system (which consisted of a dozen computers in a ring main, any one of which had access to programme material from a central store of disks) to master the range of their application as control devices. In case this may now seem mundane, let it be repeated that when it was introduced by Oundle in 1980, it was the only one in any school.

Yet impressive and terribly clever though such achievements obviously are, the new technology can only be creative in the hands of people who know how to use it responsibly. Children do not go to school merely to play with calculators or even to gain diplomas. They go to be taught the realities of life. In the end, the true purpose of education is to open up young minds to the real world they are entering. Consequently the key approach must be: 'this is the world you are going into. Have a look at it.' They have to respond to the condition of society and know how to react creatively to new situations. But they should not go out equipped merely with views and convictions provided by the school; they must also be able to think for themselves. 'If the products of the public schools haven't the capacity to think through new problems when they meet them,' says Dr Trapnell flatly, 'then the public schools ought to go out of business. The vital thing is that boys have got to have a foundation, but not necessarily an immutable one.'

To stimulate this informed awareness, a number of programmes were initiated. Some of them dealt with the need to break down barriers in Britain itself; for instance, the conflict between unions and management meant that boys should encounter 'the other side', both

in its responsible and destructive aspects. So union leaders like Vic Feather, Jack Jones, Ray Buckton and others, came and talked to the Sixth form. Though some boys objected ('What's that bloody old head man up to, asking those Commies down here?') it was better that they should meet the standpoint and aspirations of the Left (which Trapnell personally detested) at first hand rather than remain in a state of cocooned separation. Indeed one boy, who later gained a first at Oxford, was given leave from Sunday chapel to attend a union meeting. Moreover, to maintain a correct balance, the Secretary of State for Education and Derek Robinson (Red Robbo) addressed the school in successive weeks, thereby spanning the British political spectrum.

A strong social studies programme was developed, both in the shape of weekly lectures given by notable public figures, and in a variety of community projects. With these it was necessary to get away from any feeling of *noblesse oblige* or indeed 'spirit of service', which sounded priggish. The best thing to be done was to confront boys with handicapped people, and get them to work side by side. Trapnell's view was that: 'By teaching them not to be totally self-centred little brutes, these community projects helped to sensitise the boys.' And in fact some of them raised enough money to give Mencap children a memorable holiday at Oundle during the summer vacation since then repeated every year. Close links were also established with the Worcester College for the Blind, whose members were able to live in the boys' houses at Oundle, and participate in debates, concerts or even sports activities.

Opposite Barry Trapnell, headmaster from 1968-84, with the Queen Mother and OO President G.A. Wilson at the 1976 centenary celebrations of Oundle School's separation from Laxton. Left Sixth-formers on their way to classes.

Furthermore, an annual Politics Conference was initiated in 1978. That year the topic was 'The individual in a bureaucratic age'. It examined how what Lord Hailsham called 'the elected dictatorship', affected peoples' lives through its vast legislative programme. Trapnell also continued the 'Challenge of Industry' conferences, started by Michael Mills in the Dick Knight era, which studied the complexities of industrial management. Another new concept was 'Young Enterprise', whereby a group of boys set up a company to produce and market a product, in one case T-shirts with Oundle emblems on the front. The boys had to appoint directors, issue share capital, compile a balance sheet, and liquidate the firm at the end of the year. All for real, you might say.

Given the international tension at this period, and the fact that Britain could no longer assume any pre-eminence or permit any insularity, the school's activities overseas were even more valid. Usually during the half term holidays, some 40% of the Fifth form boys attended courses on East-West relations in Berlin. Other groups studied the working of the EEC, first at the European Parliament in Strasbourg, then at the European Courts of Justice in Luxembourg. One party of boys visited Hungary and Czechoslovakia to compare two Iron Curtain countries with very different social and economic systems; another went to the Soviet Union and marvelled at the skill of the Russians in combining a rigid Police State with outward openness to visitors.

Most public schools had similar schemes, of course. But it is fair to say that none was pursued with more vigour. Indeed Oundle eventually managed to initiate a glasnost of its own a couple of years before Gorbachev in the shape of the first formal link between a British school and one behind the Iron Curtain, namely the Nagy Lajos Gimnazium at Pécs in Hungary.

A series of expeditions to faraway places was all part of the same concept – that of opening boys' eyes to the world. These expeditions also drove home the message that in a rather grey period it was possible to reach out and achieve something exceptional.

The first of these globe-trotting treks explored the Equadorean Andes, and was followed by an adventure to the Hindu Kush. In this remote area, partly in Afghanistan and partly in Pakistan, the back-packers scaled peaks of 18,500 and 19,000 feet, took 6500 photographs, and carried out a number of projects, some commissioned by universities. In 1978 there were three expeditions. One involved cycling down the Nile from Alexandria to the Sudan in August, and when Trapnell received a postcard from them saying 'They think we are mad,' he replied. 'I am not surprised.' The second, to Kenya, was largely to carry out biological studies. The third was cultural – inspecting archeological sites in Greece.

Subsequent expeditions went to Sabah, Peninsular Malaysia, Papua New Guinea and South Africa. But the most exciting odyssey of all was in 1982, when Oundle became the first school in the world to be allowed by the Chinese to travel across their country. Led by Jonathan Lee, the Oundelians visited communes, schools, hospitals and so on, together with various interesting cities (one of them normally forbidden to foreigners); and were allocated several virgin peaks to climb in the northern Himalayas, of heights over 20,000 feet.

Set against such exotic backdrops, the rumblings of the youth movement at home must have seemed very trite. Yet they were at their height when Dr Trapnell took over, reflecting perhaps the student riots in Paris and the 'hot autumn' when Communism was rife in Italy. Understandably, when the whole basis of authority and discipline was under fire, many pedagogues were confused, even scared. After all, as Dr Rae has said, there is an element of bluff in the control of 600 adolescents by fifty masters. If the 600 decide to mutiny, things could become very awkward indeed.

Fortunately such a situation never arose at Oundle. Still, there were a few tricky moments. For instance, one boy tried to organise a 'no singing in chapel' strike to force his demand that two of his friends, who were being expelled for a variety of reasons, should not be. In the eighteenth century, the Headmaster of Westminster dealt with such threats very simply. He struck the fellow on the head with a club, and the mutiny subsided. Dr Trapnell stood firm too, but in a less drastic manner. He refused to see the boy, and sent him home for good that evening. (As a matter of fact, the singing strike did take place. but such was the attitude to chapel at the time that few people noticed.)

'Of course I failed many times in a new, complex and demanding situation,' admits Trapnell. 'In this case I sacked the organiser – though to be fair, he had been difficult in other ways'. As it happens, the boy in question was a brilliant student, who wanted to be a schoolmaster himself. But sadly he was emotionally unbalanced.

'It is hard to realise how mixed-up the boys were in those days,' reflects Roger Freebairn ruefully. 'The chap took upon himself more power than he could handle.'

Another boy, who had been nominated as the official representative of the NUS school branch, wanted authority in the school to devolve on to the kitchen staff, the groundsmen, and so forth. But on this occasion his demands were so ridiculous that the boys themselves laughed him out of court. However, that sort of nonsense was in the air. It was a time when the Common Room was thick with comments like 'boys fight a battle they want to lose', or 'the public schoolboy is the university student writ small'.

An example of how this defiant spirit could be handled was shown one Services Day, when a grand display of parachute drops and tank manoeuvres had been laid on. The CND supporters came with their badges, carrying flowers and voicing protests ('disgraceful to encourage an interest in killing and fighting and maiming'). But at the end of the performance the inspecting officer, General Farrar-Hockley, made a speech that practically mesmerised the school. 'You are jolly lucky,' he told them all, 'to have people like me who are willing to safeguard your freedom, even to the point of losing our own lives.' The CND supporters who had come in sneering left subdued; and roughly from that time on an interest in the services became respectable.

Barry Trapnell dealt with expressions of dissent in a pragmatic (some thought devious) way. He stood his ground while at the same time interacting with them. Thus he no longer permitted the CND badges to be worn, but allowed those who supported the movement to attend CND rallies. He allowed a group of rebellious but talented boys to form OUT (Oundle Under Threat) because of the presence of Cruise missiles at Molesworth only six miles away, and gave them a special prize on Speech Day for the responsible manner in which they had tackled the job.

He liked to work through consensus. Soon after his arrival a committee was formed with Michael Mills as chairman, to deal with the question of dress, hair styles, and general appearance of the boys; its recommendations were nearly all accepted. To make chapel more palatable ('why should I go if I don't believe?') a choice of services was given on Sundays; but to maintain order the masters had to sit with the boys. However, Roman Catholics could go to mass in the RC parish church; Jewish boys had a rabbi to come in and Muslims were expected to make their own devotions.

Carefully balanced between the need to maintain authority and the desire to move with the times, Trapnell's foremost concern was to open the school up. Accepting a realm much loved by the boys, he encouraged Pop concerts; and one Sunday, brandishing the sleeve of a King Crimson record in chapel, he preached a sermon on the lyric which was quoted earlier in this chapter.

Likewise, since informal contacts led to better control and pastoral care, he sanctioned house bars, which brought masters and boys together for a convivial brew. And, disregarding the nostrums of his predecessors, he recognised that if a boy visited a friend in another house, the world would not come to an end after all. You might say that he dealt with dissent by drawing its teeth. Not that Oundle was seriously troubled by the more strident symptoms of the youth revolution. There was an occasional little blip, nothing more.

However, money replaced youth as a hoodoo after the oil crisis of 1973. People seriously questioned whether the public schools could survive in the face of runaway inflation and the burden of taxation on the middle classes, which clearly seemed to be a political attempt to abolish them. At Oundle a most significant development was the appointment of Elliott Viney – himself an OO – as Spokesman, or liaison officer, to monitor activities and offer all the help that he could, thus symbolising a closing of the ranks between the Grocers and the school.

Despite these uncertainties, the Seventies saw a substantial improvement of the school's amenities. Soon after Trapnell's arrival a further General Appeal had been launched, which brought in over a million pounds from the OO community along with contributions from the Grocers' Company and from parents. Though this impressive sum was badly hit by inflation, it was augmented by generous donations under a new scheme known as the Annual Parents' Appeal to Year Groups.

The money was used to build married accommodation for housemasters of the remaining Field Houses. The Chemistry and Physics blocks were extended; the Physics Department was reconstructed. Some cottages at the bottom of the Bramston garden were fashioned into an attractive new residence for the Spokesman and official visitors. Some of the houses were updated, in particular New House, which was so ancient that the restoration had to be fundamental; this alone cost £400,000.

In addition, the Yarrow was brought back to life. For, sadly, Sanderson's 'Temple of Vision' had been neglected since his death, and reduced to a kind of museum with the skeleton of a horse at the entrance. When visitors enquired why it was there, they received the reply: 'Oh yes, that horse delivered the milk for eleven years in Sanderson's time.' Now the Yarrow was turned into an Art gallery, as its founder would have wished, and staged a series of exhibitions of which one of Henry Moore's work was prime event.

These transformations were financed from school funds and the big Appeal. But the new Modern Languages department in West Street, the Micro-electronics centre, the athletics track and new games field, eight new hard tennis courts and three new squash courts, were funded by the APA, which, along with a massive contribution from the Rudolphe Stahl estate, also paid for the Stahl Theatre. (Rudolphe Stahl, a brilliant inventor who went penniless to America, worked with Henry Ford and designed the Maxwell car, which later became the first Chrysler. He spent a year as a boy at Oundle in 1900-1901, and believed that the impact of the Sanderson outlook had so profoundly affected his life that by the time he died in 1975 at the age of ninety-one he had given over £400,000 to the school.)

Cleverly evolved by converting the old Congregational church, the Stahl Theatre was opened in February 1980 by HRH Princess Alice, and heralded a new era for Oundle drama. Under the direction of John Harrison, and staffed largely by some seventy boys it is administered as far as possible like a professional theatre. Apart from housing the school's own productions, it puts on a wide range of plays and other shows – including mime, puppets, dance, and even small-scale opera – performed by visiting companies. With its permanent stage and 300 seats it fulfilled a long-felt need, and soon became a theatrical landmark in the region.

These continuous building operations (which as a matter of fact show no signs of abating) serve to focus attention on the man who has the day to day responsibility of keeping everything moving – namely the Bursar. For over the years the Bursar has become an increasingly important member of the community.

Bursars have been key figures since the Middle Ages. But earlier in this century, when life was simpler than it is now, the Bursar was little more than a glorified accountant. Sanderson acted as his own bursar, which is perhaps why Fisher appointed G.S. Rees in 1928 to 'earth things down'. In my day (the late Thirties) he appeared to be a shadowy presence who lived in a dingy office in the back of beyond. Actually, of course, he was a vital element in the school's economy, whose routine tasks ranged from the care of school property and the control of all purchases to the supervision of non-teaching staff and even the accommodation of guests. Apart from preparing the accounts, he had to keep an eye on the various building projects, which were numerous and varied.

For over thirty years Grif Rees responded to the cry 'Where's the Bursar?' when any crisis arose. If a boarding house caught fire (as Sidney did in 1938): if an aeroplane landed on the cricket ground, or a lorry smashed the paved way to the chapel just before a Royal Personage was due to tread on it, he had to cope with the problem. It is not surprising, therefore, that the Bursar's job was upgraded when Gim Milton took over in 1960; or that the enormous increase in routine administrative work as the school grew to nearly 800 boys made it necessary to appoint an estates Bursar as his deputy. (At Harrow there are four Bursars, at Eton, five.)

Indeed, along with the headmaster, the Bursar became a governors' appointment, and as such ranked second in the hierarchy. If Barry Trapnell was managing director, Gim Milton was the financial director, responsible for finance and procurement. True, the Bursar's position in the chain of command was ambiguous in some ways; being responsible both to the headmaster and the governing body. But as Trapnell was the first to agree, this was not without its advantages in acting as a break – though more often a spur – to his more extravagant schemes, and in dealing with the financial implications.

Today, some ten years later, and in the McMurray era, Colin Cheshire has to handle an annual turnover of seven million pounds. He directs a staff of 350, which comprises, among others, 34 in the Clerk of Works department; a catering manager with 20 cooks and 20

159

washers-up; 12 domestics in each boarding house; 17 groundsmen, and all the secretarial staff. 'Flexibility and patience are the cry,' he says, and since he has to report on practically everything other than the academic side (including the Bookshop) it is appropriate that Bursar should now be written with a capital B.

To mention (parenthetically) that Colin Cheshire was also Manager of the Great Britain Rifle team which recently made a hash of the Aussies Down Under would be to get ahead of our story. So let us return to the late Seventies when Oundle was not doing so badly on the sporting side either.

For one thing, the Cricket XI remained unbeaten for three years running (1976-78) and in 1979 three of the team went on to obtain Blues at Oxford and Cambridge – the first time any school had obtained this number in one year since 1952.

The Tennis VI was unbeaten for four successive years, and one of their number, A.D. Smith of Bramston, who had been the under-sixteen national champion in 1978, was elected Schoolboy Tennis Player of the Year in 1979, receiving his award from Mark Cox on the centre court at Wimbledon on semi-finals day. The Athletics team lost only one match in four years, and was ranked second in the country in 1979, when concurrently the Fives team was in the finals of the Schools competition. Themselves undefeated for two years, the Oundle golfers were runners-up in the Public Schools Championship of 1981, a year in which OOs had four Blues at squash, as well as providing the captain of the Oxford team.

And so on, and so on. The litany was unending. For if Oundle rugger failed to reach its former peaks – though half of the school's twelve XVs were undefeated in 1978, and the First XV ended 1981 with three wins over traditional rivals – it was perhaps because so many of the senior boys were concentrating on the newer sports. Indeed the devotees of clay-pigeon shooting were British School champions in 1981, and one of them became European Junior Champion. At Bisley and other venues, trophies were regularly won; the swimming team was undefeated, and six of them swam the Channel in 9 hours 38 minutes, a very fast time given the highly adverse conditions. (In fact on the way home in a plane piloted by Mike Skliros, an OO chaplain in the RAF, the cloud was so thick that it was necessary to fly about 20 feet above the motorway. Barry Trapnell thought this splendid fun; but the chaplain discovered that when you are in grave danger, praying is not the first thing you think about.)

All in all, then, Oundle completed its fifth century of existence conscious of being at the height of its vigour, enlivened by useful enterprise and adventure, laced with academic success, and maybe grudgingly (though probably gratefully) acknowledging the hands that had successively steered the school to this meridian.

Ruthless in the sense that he would stand no nonsense and was impatient with fools, the man who was now handing over the helm had been an innovator of genius, as the governors had spotted from the start. Combining the detachment of an analytic scientist with the verve of a triple Blue, Barry Trapnell had the ability to keep many balls in play at the same time. He made some brilliant appointments; even so, he was not entirely popular with the staff, many of whom found him too galvanic for comfort, too much of a bulldozer.

Barry Trapnell himself would have said that he was an enabler – someone who helps others to do the job. An idea would be put forward, for example John Harrison's notion of the theatre, and Barry enabled it to be set up. Often he expanded the idea itself. Jonathan Lee, who was thinking of taking an expedition to North Wales, was told: 'I like the thought. But why don't you go further afield – say to China?' And he knew how to produce swift action. When John Coll and Charles Sweeten suggested the first micro-electronics lab in Britain, Barry convinced the governors and got the money, enabling the project to go immediately ahead.

He also understood how necessary it was to shatter prejudice and appeal to the new middle class that was emerging in Britain – brash, if you like, but open, adaptive, and able to think on its feet. At the same time he knew how to cast the net wide, and by projecting a dynamic and unstuffy image of Oundle abroad, to build up a remarkable connection with many of the top families in South-east Asia.

'People called me an opportunist,' he agrees, 'But surely that is only seeing what history is presenting you with. You say to yourself: "that would be good – and we can do it!" You see, the nice thing about running an independent school is that if you can persuade your governors, you can get things done. You can move quickly and well and therefore creatively. From the day of conception, to completion, the micro-electronics project took only four months'.

In brief, if Stainforth was Oundle's Monty, Trapnell was Oundle's Maggie. In many senses he shares the same galvanic convictions as Margaret Thatcher, and on the small stage of Oundle he imposed them ruthlessly. Like the Prime Minister, he sought to redress the balance between non-productive permissiveness and dynamic achievement. What is more, he succeeded. For sixteen years he *was* Oundle, seizing every opportunity that could be used for the benefit of the school.

In this he was playing from strength. For clearly the great advantage that the independent schools enjoy today is that they are not hampered by bureaucratic interference. They can act on their own. And because of this they are of value to the whole community.

However, it has to be admitted that most of the established public schools failed to make best use of this advantage during the Seventies. They continued to inhabit a world of their own. A few followed Oundle's example and pioneered Nuffield Science Courses in Physics, Chemistry, Biology or Modern Mathematics. Others, like Marlborough, embarked on business studies. But that was about all.

The fashionable issue, after John Dancy had introduced girls into Marlborough in 1968, was undoubtedly desegregation. At first this was seen as a liberating measure, but once inflation began to bite it became increasingly attractive for purely economic reasons.

Right *David McMurray, headmaster from 1984. From 1990 the Oundle School would be taking girls, as Laxton was since 1986. Above Laxton Sixth-former Victoria Hunt, with her team mates, wins the UK Federation Business and Professional Women's Public Speaking Contest in 1988.*

Motivated by a shortfall in the number of boys, and to a lesser extent by the belief that the atmosphere would be healthier with females around, the schools began to open their doors to girls. Some went fully coeducational; others simply admitted them into the Sixth form.

Oakham went the whole hog with considerable success. Uppingham, more cautiously, turned the sanatorium (which was the school's greatest white elephant) into a girls' boarding house. Taunton took over a neighbouring girls' school. In one way or another fully a quarter of the independent schools were admitting girls by 1979, and in due course John Rae scooped the lot by appointing a black girl as Head of School at Westminster.

All this was admirable, (even if still somewhat cosmetic.) But it tended to mask the fact that – either through complacency or sheer lack of confidence – the independent schools were letting the Seventies slip by without making any noticeable progress in other directions.

Having a school that was overflowing, and other priorities which he considered more important, Trapnell rejected any idea of introducing co-education to Oundle. 'I preferred glasnost to girls,' he said, 'I suppose it's a matter of temperament.' He was running a tight ship, and intended to keep it that way. Always pragmatic, often authoritarian, he concentrated on taking Oundle to the top. And, to his credit, he succeeded. It was left to David McMurray, when he took over in 1984, to capitalise on this success and endow it, moreover, with the endearing quality of compassion.

EPILOGUE

AT THIS POINT, tidily rounding off half a millenium of recorded history, the story of Oundle should logically end; for the moving present cannot be viewed in historical perspective. However a few parting remarks may not be out of place, for already, during the four years that he has been in command, David McMurray has taken several momentous steps which will alter and enhance the character of the school.

Firstly, in tune with European thinking, he has abolished corporal punishment; and by removing the pedagogue's traditional weapon has put an end to the charge of institutionalised cruelty which has for so long blemished the image of Anglo-Saxon education. Coercion has been replaced by collaboration.

Having launched a successful Appeal which brought in the necessary funds, he has built a magnificent new sports hall; converted the fifty-year-old gymnasium into a striking new library; and provided an entire new Physics block – all of which are now completed.

Perhaps most important of all, he is bringing in the girls, and thus diluting the all-pervasive masculinity of the place. Who knows, perhaps Oundle will lose some of its time-honoured characteristics as a result. But the atmosphere is bound to become more relaxed, more in harmony with the world of today, without losing any of its underlying vitality.

For these significant developments, I salute both the Governors and the new Head.

Having personally known five headmasters of Oundle, I must stress that each of them made his own distinctive contribution to the school. Dr Fisher's regime, for instance, produced what was probably the most outstanding generation of OOs, which included 14 Fellows of the Royal Society, along with numerous High Court judges and university professors; the Head of the Metropolitan Police (whose long-jump record still stands), a plethora of top industrialists and even the odd cabinet minister. However, I would suggest that Dr Trapnell had the greatest impact by opening up the school to the world. Together with Sanderson, he must rate as Oundle's most notable Head. Yet I have an idea that future historians will bracket David McMurray with these two great names. For he too is an innovator, with a style which goes with the time: informal and relaxed, pithy and humorous. No one has done more in so short a period.

He was headmaster of his old school, Loretto, when the governing body of the Grocers' Company asked him (for he did not apply) to come to Oundle. And right from the outset both he and his wife Toni dispensed with headmagisterial pomp. Beautifully redecorated, their home at Cobthorne has become the welcoming heart of Oundle today; its doors are

women. As a result, Oundle boys will have women as working colleagues at all levels in their later lives – and are likely to have female bosses too. Many of the feeder schools and all the universities are now open to both sexes. So the decision to take in girls was a wise and inescapable one absolutely in keeping with Oundle's reputation, earned in Sanderson's day, and jealously maintained, for providing an education which is fully relevant to the world outside its walls. As David McMurray has said, 'in order to ensure that the transition is effected with thoroughness and excellence. I emphasis that the qualities which we seek to foster – sound values, a clear understanding of the nature of today's world, the ability to take responsibility and adapt in a period of change, an understanding of technological development, a respect for learning and ideas – these qualities we shall continue to develop in our pupils.'

What he might have added, but didn't, is that in the highly competitive situation of today there is great value in the simple act of paying fees. For to overcome a £7000 obstacle, standards have to be kept high. Because of that contract, a direct responsibility is placed on the school to fulfil its obligations. It might even be said that the independent schools are helped by the vulnerability of the state sector to anxiety in people's minds over academic standards.

In a free market situation, competition keeps the public schools on their toes. Indeed their freedom and quickness of movement is a parameter of quality. They cannot afford to get left behind in the race. They have to stay in front. And this is where Oundle has always excelled. 'The vocation of Oundle,' says Elliott Viney, a former Spokesman for the Grocers' Company, 'is to be ahead of its time.'

Not so long ago I was invited by the Vice-Provost of Eton to have lunch in College. Afterwards we went upstairs to the great Library, and there, as I was poring over a Gutenberg Bible lying casually on the table, we were joined by the headmaster's wife.

'Oundle!' she exclaimed after I had been introduced. 'D'you know, in my opinion Oundle is the best school in England today.'

I blush to quote so generous a tribute, and from such a source, too. But it makes a good ending. And, who knows, she may even be right . . . . Certainly this view was confirmed by Jock Burnet, editor of the *Public Schools Book* for the past forty years: 'At the top of the list I'd put Oundle and . . . . ', he told me at a dinner recently.

Perhaps I should leave it to youto fill in the blank.

_____ APPENDIX ONE _____
LAXTON SCHOOL

FOR NEARLY A HUNDRED YEARS after the split in 1876, Laxton School tended to be regarded as a kind of day-boy extension to Oundle (although to purists it remained the true lineal descendant of the Founder's endowed grammar school). Yet Laxton School continued to have a identity of its own, as Kim Morrison, the Senior History Master, explains:

When Bob Whitby took over in 1968, Laxton School was the only grammar school in the Oundle area and so about one half of the boys came as 11-plus examination successes. Fees for the remaining pupils were extremely low and numbers were around the one hundred mark. Unlike his predecessors, who acted as Master-in-charge under the Oundle School Headmaster, Whitby was designated as Headmaster of Laxton, and this he most certainly was. A stern disciplinarian, a keen games player and, later, the Prince of Wales' housemaster at Gordonstoun, he had that rare ability to encourage and galvanise people into outstanding effort. One remembers a soccer match at Huntingdon, when Laxton were trailing by four goals with a quarter of an hour to go. Suddenly Bob Whitby appeared on the touchline. A few stentorian words from him and heads were raised, legs ran faster, and in no time three goals had been pulled back. In 1969 and 1970, for the first time in living memory, Laxton School won the Inter-House singing competition as they rode the wave of new enthusiasm.

During this period Prince Charles was a regular private visitor to the Whitby household, which was situated in the main school building; and the Laxton Headmaster was a guest at Caernarvon Castle when the heir-apparent was installed as Prince of Wales. Much to his delight, Whitby sat in the _front_ row of guests, while the Prime Minister, Harold Wilson, was only in the _second_ row.

With numbers increasing and with the advent of a state comprehensive school in the town further changes had to be made. Firstly, as the flow of 11-plus candidates dried up, and with it state support, fees had to be greatly increased. Secondly, the main school building was not needed in its entirety and so the Headmaster moved to the recently acquired White Lion, a delightful old timber and stone residence almost opposite the school buildings. A new dining room was built on to the Oundle School Refectory as Laxton Senior and Junior schools outgrew the old dining area adjoining the school.

Bob Whitby moved on to the headmastership of Bembridge School, Isle-of-Wight, in 1974 and was replaced by John Simpson from Bishop's Stortford. Over the next nine years the Long Room, the Cloisters and all the rooms in the house were refurbished and re-allocated. The two rooms which for some time had been dormitories for Bramston House boarders, were transformed into classrooms; the bedrooms and bachelor flat became common rooms as did the old kitchen and dining room. John Simpson introduced an efficient tutorial system and greatly increased the sporting options and coaching facilities so that cricket in particular advanced into a golden age where victory was frequent and defeat rare.

The academic shape of Laxton School changed considerably in the early 1970s as a process of closer integration with Oundle's curriculum began. Whereas there had been four separate Laxton forms, the Third and Fourth forms were absorbed by Oundle School and there only remained Laxton One and Two which ran parallel -- and in some subjects were setted with -- the Berrystead forms. More and more these first two forms consisted of a majority of boys from Laxton Junior School, pupils from whose Sixth form crossed North Street once a week to share in a assembly in the Long Room. The standard of the entrance examination was raised and Laxton boys have regularly gained places at Oxford and Cambridge.

The closer links with Oundle manifested themselves in other ways as Laxton pupils joined in productions at the Stahl Theatre and Laxton sportsmen ran, swam or shot for highly successful Oundle teams. At one stage the two Taylor brothers from Laxton held nineteen of the twenty-two Oundle swimming records, and Stefan Glaysher was Oundle cross-country captain. In this closer linking of the two schools, many Laxton pupils were awarded Oundle School prizes for academic and artistic achievement and, although there are traditionally two speech days in the Summer and Michaelmas terms respectively, the Oundle Schools became more closely interwoven than at any time since the split between the two in 1876.

David Richardson came from Rugby School in the summer of 1983 to replace John Simpson as Headmaster and to him fell the task of paving the way for entry of girls into Laxton School. With hindsight, it is easy to look upon such a step as inevitable, but at the time it required considerable planning and forethought. Separate common rooms and facilities were allocated and in the Michaelmas term of 1986 the first tentative steps towards co-education at Laxton -- and subsequently, Oundle -- were taken, as eight girls were accepted into the Lower Sixth form as day pupils. A similar number were enrolled in the following year to bring a refreshing new dimension to the school. In the Michaelmas term of 1989 day-girls will be accepted into the school at junior levels.

Even before the addition of girls to the school register, numbers at Laxton had risen steadily in the 1970s and 1980s (from some 100 to 150 over a period of twenty years), as demand for independent education increased. One aspect of this expansion has been the ever-widening area from which pupils are drawn, although David Richardson was careful to protect the original aim of Laxton School to provide an education for the scholars of Oundle town. Emphasis continued to be given to providing a worthwhile and fulfilling day-school education through a full sporting diary and a programme of drama, music and other social events. On the financial side the school has sought to attract local pupils of high academic potential by scholarships, bursaries and assisted places, striving continually to strengthen its links with the

168

town, not least because of the ever-growing presence of many Old Laxtonians in local enterprises.

Since Tom Stretton breathed new life into the Old Laxtonian Club in the 1950s, the club has flourished. A highlight of the sports fixture list each term is the encounter between the school and the Old Boys, be it at soccer, hockey or cricket: decade by decade honours have remained about even, although it is fair to say that lately the school elevens have more than held their own, especially at cricket. If the school has definitely had the upper hand in recent years, defeats are soon forgotten as members move on to the Old Boys' dinner in the evening, held now, significantly, in Great Hall with the Master of the Grocers' Company as chief guest. The Old Boys, too, had to examine their 'men only' policy when Miss Pat Ogden was appointed as Head of the Laxton Junior School and when women teachers became tutors at the senior school. It was not always easy for the more senior Old Boys to adapt to, for them, radical changes, but in due course all Laxtonians have come to accept the changing direction of the school.

As Laxton School prepares itself for the twenty-first century, it is fitting to recall the two men who, between them, were most responsible for plotting its path through the twentieth century. In 1979 S.J.J. 'Quack' Leech died, having retired in 1952 after thirty years as Master-in-charge. He was followed by Tom Stretton who was in charge for the next sixteen years. Tom died in 1986 at a time when his own grandson was a boarder at Dryden House. A memorial tablet to Leech on the wall of the Long Room, together with artists' sketches of both himself and Tom Stretton are fitting reminders of their contribution to Laxton School.

Many of the major boarding schools have day-house or day-boy sections, but the Laxton School-Oundle School relationship is unique, and difficult to define. 'Integration with independence' might be the best description of the association between the two as they move towards the next century. Oundle School will itself accept girls from 1990 and this might seem an appropriate moment to merge Laxton School entirely with its larger partner. But, to anyone who has ever attended an assembly, a school play, or a social function in the magnificent Laxton Long Room, steeped as it is in four hundred and fifty years of academic tradition and progress, or participated in the Carol Service with its family warmth and wonderful singing, there can be little doubt that the two schools, which are so close in many ways, will best continue if they preserve their present traditions.

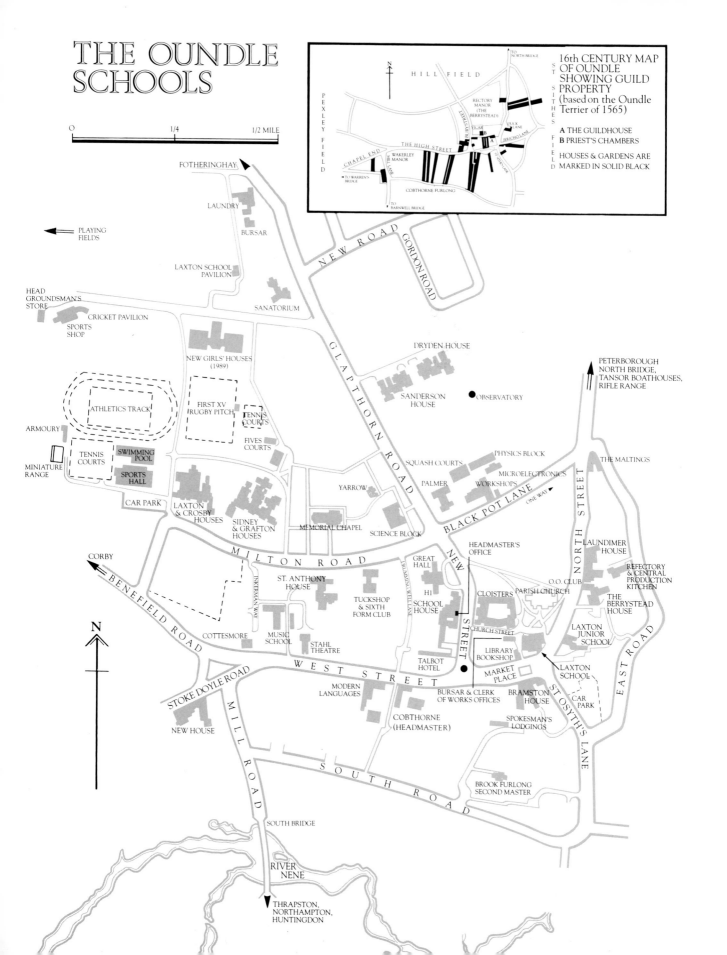

THE MAIN ENGLISH AND SCOTTISH SCHOOLS MENTIONED IN THIS BOOK

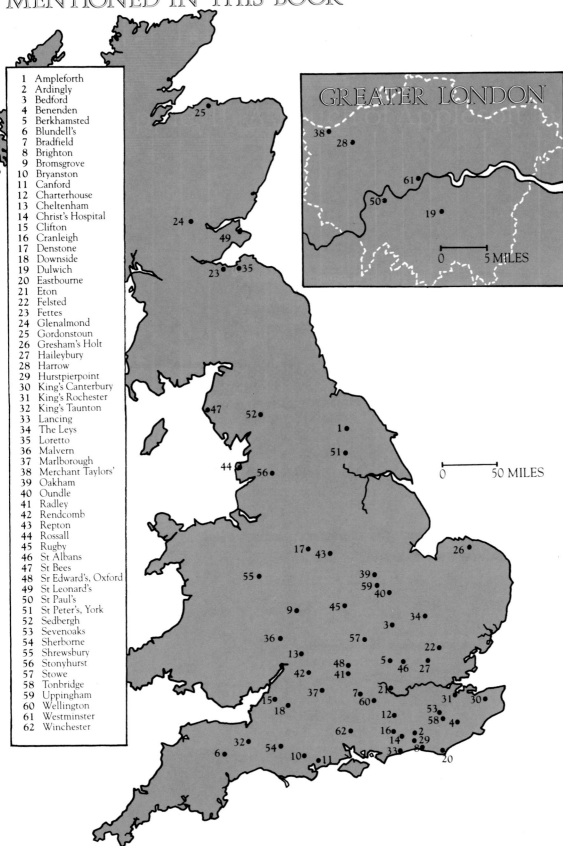

1 Ampleforth
2 Ardingly
3 Bedford
4 Benenden
5 Berkhamsted
6 Blundell's
7 Bradfield
8 Brighton
9 Bromsgrove
10 Bryanston
11 Canford
12 Charterhouse
13 Cheltenham
14 Christ's Hospital
15 Clifton
16 Cranleigh
17 Denstone
18 Downside
19 Dulwich
20 Eastbourne
21 Eton
22 Felsted
23 Fettes
24 Glenalmond
25 Gordonstoun
26 Gresham's Holt
27 Haileybury
28 Harrow
29 Hurstpierpoint
30 King's Canterbury
31 King's Rochester
32 King's Taunton
33 Lancing
34 The Leys
35 Loretto
36 Malvern
37 Marlborough
38 Merchant Taylors'
39 Oakham
40 Oundle
41 Radley
42 Rendcomb
43 Repton
44 Rossall
45 Rugby
46 St Albans
47 St Bees
48 Sr Edward's, Oxford
49 St Leonard's
50 St Paul's
51 St Peter's, York
52 Sedbergh
53 Sevenoaks
54 Sherborne
55 Shrewsbury
56 Stonyhurst
57 Stowe
58 Tonbridge
59 Uppingham
60 Wellington
61 Westminster
62 Winchester

GREATER LONDON

0   5 MILES

0   50 MILES

FOUNDATION DATES

Oundle's recorded history begins with the chantry school in 1485, which was re-endowed as a grammar school by Sir William Laxton in 1556 and became a public school in 1876. Here, in chronological order, are the foundation dates of some other well-known schools:

600	King's Canterbury	1561	Merchant Taylors'	1850	Bradfield
604	King's Rochester	1564	Felsted	1853	Epsom
627	St Peter's York	1565	Highgate	1856	Wellington
914	Warwick	1567	Rugby	1859	Oratory
948	St Albans	1571	Harrow	1861	Beaumont
1090	Lincoln	1583	St Bees	1862	Clifton
1150	Bedford	1584	Oakham	1862	Haileybury
1256	Norwich	1584	Uppingham	1862	Malvern
1382	Winchester	1596	Whitgift	1863	Cranleigh
1400	Ipswich	1597	Aldenham	1863	St Edward's Oxford
1414	Durham	1604	Blundell's	1865	Framlingham
1432	Sevenoaks	1611	Charterhouse	1866	Trent
1440	Eton	1619	Dulwich	1867	Eastbourne
1495	Magdalen College School	1628	Heriot's Edinburgh	1867	Bishops Stortford
1509	St Paul's	1723	Watson's Edinburgh	1868	Monkton Combe
1512	Giggleswick	1793	Downside	1868	Denstone
1515	Manchester Grammar	1794	Stonyhurst	1870	Fettes
1520	Cranbrook	1802	Ampleforth	1871	Dover
1525	Sedbergh	1807	Mill Hill	1875	The Leys
1541	Berkhamsted	1824	Edinburgh Academy	1880	Wrekin
1543	Dauntsey's	1827	Loretto	1886	Dean Close
1550	Sherborne	1841	Cheltenham	1893	Bedales
1552	Christ's Hospital	1841	Glenalmond	1903	Douai
1552	King Edward's Birmingham	1843	Marlborough	1905	R.N.C. Dartmouth
1552	Shrewsbury	1844	Rossall	1912	Imperial Service College
1553	Bromsgrove	1845	Brighton	1920	Rendcomb
1553	Tonbridge	1845	Glasgow Academy	1923	Canford
1555	Gresham's Holt	1847	Radley	1923	Stowe
1557	Repton	1847	Taunton	1928	Bryanston
1560	Westminster	1848	Lancing	1934	Gordonstoun

SELECTED BIBLIOGRAPHY

Annan, Noel *Roxburgh of Stowe* Longmans, 1965

Armitage, W.G.H. *Four Hundred Years of English Education* CUP, 1965

Bamford, T. *The Rise of the Public Schools* Nelson, 1967

Barnard, H.C. *A Short History of English Education from 1760-1944* Univ. of London, 1947

Betjeman, John *Summoned by Bells* John Murray, 1960

Blumenau, Ralph *A History of Malvern College* Macmillan, 1965

Chandos, John *Boys Together: English Public Schools 1800-1864* OUP, 1985

Clarke, A.K. *A History of Cheltenham Ladies' College* Faber, 1953

Collins, W.L. *The Public Schools* Blackwood, 1867

Dahl, Roald *Boy* Penguin, 1986

Dancy, John *The Public Schools and the Future* Faber, 1963

Field, John *The Kings' Nurseries* James & James, 1987

Gaythorne-Hardy, Jonathan *The Public School Phenomenon* Penguin, 1979

Gaunt, H.C.A. *Two Exiles* Sampson Lowe, 1946

Greenall, R.J. *A History of Northamptonshire and the Soke of Peterborough* Phillimore & Co. Ltd., 1979

Honey, J. de S. *Tom Brown's Universe* Millington, 1977

Lambert, Royston *The Hothouse Society* Weidenfeld, 1968

Lawrence, P.S.H. (Ed.) *The Encouragement of Learning* Russell, 1980

Leach A. F. *Schools of Medieval England* London, 1915

Mack, E.C. *Public Schools and British Opinion since 1860* Columbia Univ. NY, 1941

Marshall, Arthur *Life's Rich Pageant* Hamish Hamilton, 1982

Matthews, Bryan *By God's Grace* Whitehall Press, 1984

Ogilvie, Vivian *The English Public School* Batsford, 1957

Ollard, Richard *An English Education, a Perspective of Eton* Collins, 1982

Percival, Alicia *The Origins of the Head Masters' Conference* John Murray, 1969

Rae, John *The Public School Revolution, Britain's Independent Schools 1964-1979* Faber, 1981©

Rodgers, John *Old Public Schools of England* Batsford, 1938

Shiels, W.J. *The Puritans in the Diocese of Peterborough, 1558-1610* Northamptonshire Record Society, 1979

Simpson, J. Hope *Rugby since Arnold* Macmillan, 1967

Tozer, Malcolm *Physical Education at Thring's Uppingham* Uppingham, 1976

Tozer, Malcolm *Sanderson of Oundle* Chatto & Windus, 1923

Walker, W.G. *A History of the Oundle Schools* London, 1956

Wells, H.G. *The Story of a Great Headmaster* Chatto & Windus, 1924

Youings, J. *Sixteenth-century England* Penguin, 1984

INDEX

Note: Bold figures indicate illustrative matter within text.